Love Trumps Grief
The Fight to Save Our Sons and the Gift That Saved Us

Kristin Akin

First published by Dog Ear Publishing
4010 W. 86th Street, Ste H
Indianapolis, IN 46268
www.dogearpublishing.net

ISBN: 978-1-4575-1256-8

Editing by Eva van Emden

Cover photo by Karen Hendrix

This book is printed on acid-free paper.

Printed in the United States of America

Dedication

*To my children: Matthew Austin, Andrew Preston
and William Clayton; the most precious gifts
I could have ever been given. I love you the most!*

Acknowledgments

I began writing this book about two-thirds of the way into our journey. I am not sure what made me begin, as writing a book has never been on my bucket list. The title changed three times, and I can't begin to count how many times I started over until something finally stuck, and I was able to move past the first few pages. But as time passed, it became more and more clear that this was something I had to do, despite it being the second most difficult thing I have ever done. The only thing harder than writing about it was living it.

Let me state for the record: it was not cathartic, as everyone asked and assumed. When I talked to my editor about this she made a very interesting point: often when people write a memoir they are sharing a family or personal secret, and the writing is cathartic because they are finally letting their secret out. But in this story, there is no secret; just a horrible tragedy, and retelling it does not make it easier or less painful. It was difficult, as I am not a writer by trade and doing this did not come naturally. It was excruciatingly painful to dredge up the details and write and rewrite them over and over. But in the end, it was me and only me who could write this story, and so no matter what, I had to keep plugging away. My hope is that sharing our story will help people. The lessons are many, and what you take away will depend on what is happening in your life. Charlie Brown said it best: in the book of life, the answers are not in the back.

In the course of thirty-three months, three hospitals and four bone marrow transplants I crossed paths with countless doctors, nurses, therapists and every kind of staff, from the cashier in the cafeteria to the housekeepers. I could never mention everyone because that list would be a small book in itself. I offer my most sincere and heartfelt thank-yous to each of you who came into my life and offered part of yourself to me and my family during the worst possible experience. I still keep in touch with several of our nurses, therapists and doctors. A smile, a hug, a listening ear — these were just a few of the things you offered to me daily and that was part of what kept me going. Thank you.

To all the families of critically ill children that I lived with: I have a magnet with a picture of a hand and a small bird sitting, resting on the hand. The quote under the picture says, "We give comfort and receive comfort, sometimes at the same time." That sums up our lives perfectly. We spoke the same language, we shared the same fears and ultimately fought the same battle, even if the disease was not the same. We all wanted the same thing: a healthy child. Like soldiers at war, we lived in the trenches together, doing what we had to do to help each other through the scariest and most painful times in our lives. Thank you.

A special thank-you to my parents. I have been blessed with two loving and supportive parents who have stood by my side throughout my life in any and all my endeavors. Thank you for loving me unconditionally.

To my dear friends — you know who you are: thank you for calling, coming by, sending packages, making food, and most importantly, loving me and my family. You kept me going in ways you will never know. I often wonder why you stuck by me through this nightmare that just didn't seem to end, but I am eternally grateful that you did.

To my oldest, dearest and best friend Mel (G.): it started at the corner of Fairway Lake and Westpar over twenty-five years ago. We have something that most people dream about — thank you. You are the definition of loyal and I am honored to call you my best friend. Thank you for everything you did and continue to do. — O.

To my husband and life partner, Justin: we both know that how we met was written long ago like the rest of our journey. I could never have made it through without you. Our boys have the most loving, patient and amazing dad in the world, and for that I thank you. We have weathered a storm most people could never imagine, but I know that now our future is bright. I love you.

Chapter 1

The longer we dwell on our misfortunes the greater is their power to harm us.
—Voltaire

January 2009

We knew it was going to be a long day, driving six hours each way. But making the round trip to Cincinnati Children's Hospital was the easy part. Meeting with doctors to discuss Andrew's options — that was exhausting.

When Andrew was initially diagnosed with hemophagocytic lymphohistiocytosis (HLH), we did what most parents would do: got online and Googled it. There wasn't a lot of information out there on this rare immune deficiency, but we quickly found the Histiocytosis Association of America. We also learned that Dr. Edwards at Cincinnati Children's Hospital was the world renowned expert so we emailed her to get a second opinion.

We called her and discussed the proposed plan of care Andrew would receive here in St. Louis. Without seeing him in person she was hesitant to say much, but she confirmed that at St. Louis Children's Hospital they would use the 2004 HLH protocol, just as they would at Cincinnati. At the time our knowledge of the disease and the treatment was very limited and the choice seemed simple. If the same treatment was going to be used at both hospitals, why leave St. Louis Children's to go to Cincinnati Children's? But now, after our visit, all I can say is, damn, were we wrong. I will forever regret not going to Cincinnati from the start. While I usually say *you only know what you know*, that's not good enough in the case of my son's life.

After two visits to Cincinnati and meeting with the team, seeing the facilities and discussing the options, we know it is time to transfer Andrew's care. I can't help but think — maybe hope is a better word — that 2009 is finally going to be our year. It has to be. We are overdue for some good news, for things to finally go our way. During our visits with the team we made it clear that if they don't truly think Andrew has a good chance of surviving, then we don't want to subject him to any more treatment. They assured us that they felt Andrew was not at that point, but they understood where we were coming from and would let us know if we got there.

It seems surreal to hear myself talk about *if* he makes it. All along it has always been *when* he makes it, *when* he is a long-term survivor, *when* he gets to meet his donor, but now, after two failed bone marrow transplants and countless complications, I am starting to realize that *if* is the operative word. At this point, I have eighteen months' worth of experience living in the hospital. I have watched kids die that we all said could never — would never — and conversely, I have seen children so sick their only hope was an intervention by God who not only made it but went on to thrive. No one can know what will happen.

As with any big decision, I am feeling a myriad of emotions. I am hopeful about what lies ahead for Andrew, yet scared of the unknown. Over the last eighteen months, I have formed special bonds with so many people at St. Louis: everyone from our chaplain to the housekeepers. They have been there for me in my darkest moments of despair and they've helped me celebrate even the smallest victories along our path. Therapists, nurses, Child Life Services: these are the people I have lived with, shared my life with and shared my deepest fears with. But as loving and dedicated and intelligent as they are, they don't make the decisions about Andrew's care, and that is why we have to leave and head to Cincinnati. We must do everything in our power to try and give Andrew the best chance of beating HLH.

"Let me see that e-mail again," I say to Justin.

> Dear Mr. Akin,
> We have some preliminary results I would like to discuss with you and your wife. Would you let me know when I may call? These results are somewhat complicated and are potentially quite meaningful. Before we talk, I just wanted to let you know that I am going to strongly recommend that all four of you (and especially Andrew) come to see me in Cincinnati next Wednesday (again). I really think it would be in your best interest.
> Dr. Oliver.

How can he send an e-mail like this and then not think we will want to talk to him right away? We have to find out what he is talking about. I immediately call the hospital and leave a message, my heart racing. While we wait impatiently for him to call back, I get another idea. I call Abigail, our bone marrow coordinator — I bet she can help. And lo and behold, I am right. She hears the panic in my voice and within minutes Dr. Oliver calls us.

My heart is pounding, and I have broken out into a cold sweat as I pace back and forth in the basement. Justin is upstairs in our bedroom so we can be on a conference call. In the background I can hear Matthew with the babysitter on the main floor, running around. We were about to go out to dinner for my thirty-fourth birthday, and now we are hearing the most devastating news we have ever heard. I continue to listen until there is a pause, and the doctor asks if we have any questions.

I try to recapture what I think I just heard.

"You are saying that the cause of Andrew's HLH is a relatively new-found X-linked mutation, and that Matthew has it too? And even though Matthew is healthy right now, at some point he is going to get HLH as well? And to top it off, this mutation came from me? I gave it to my sons?"

"Yes, you are correct, Mrs. Akin; however, we cannot tell you when or what virus will trigger the disease. At some point, Matthew will be exposed to something that will activate HLH. I am so sorry to have to call and tell you this. I am sure you have a lot of questions, so please feel free to ask me now or call me when you have had some time to let things sink in. At some point, we would like to get samples from the other women on your side, Mom, to see if we can pinpoint where the mutation began."

"OK," I say in disbelief. "We will call you tomorrow." We hang up.

I fall to my knees, sobbing uncontrollably. I hear the basement door open and feel Justin's arms around me.

"Come here, stand up."

"No, I can't. I can't believe this. I don't understand what just happened."

"I don't really understand myself."

"This is all my fault," I sob. "I gave my most precious gifts, the only things that matter to me in this life, a mutation that causes this horrific disease? And now it's only a matter of time before Matthew gets sick too? I cannot believe this. How can God let this happen? Am I that bad of a person that I deserve this much pain and heartache? Why can't this nightmare fall on me? Why my children? I just don't understand."

We stand there for what seems like an eternity, holding each other and crying. Finally, Justin steps back, takes my hand and starts to pull me towards him as he walks towards the basement stairs.

"Kristin, we need to talk and we don't want Matthew to see us like this or hear any of it. I know we're not in the mood, but let's get out of the house."

I stand there crying and don't say a word for a while. I finally wipe away the tears and snot and start up the basement stairs behind Justin. I think I am in shock. I reassure our sitter, Emily, one of the very few people who we trust to watch Andrew, that we will be back soon. She can see I have been crying but knows not to ask now. I kiss Matthew good-bye and hope he doesn't notice my face, and then I lean in to kiss Andrew, who tries to grab my hair, all the while laughing. My boys, my beautiful, wonderful boys.

As we pull out of the garage, we look at each other and our tears begin to flood the car. I immediately put the window down, even though it's winter and very cold outside. I need the air to breathe. I squeeze Justin's hand and try to say the words, "I'm sorry, I'm just so sorry!"

Chapter 2

Every child born into the world is a new thought of God,
an ever fresh and radiant possibility.
—Kate Douglas Wiggin

August 2007

inally, home sweet home. After being away, for even a few days, I always cherish coming home. As soon as my ob-gyn had confirmed my pregnancy with Andrew I had started asking — begging — to have a C-section, and boy, was I glad I did. Thus far, the recovery had been so much less painful than my delivery of Matthew and much more what I expected. Sitting on our couch in the family room felt comfortable, cozy and familiar. I cradled my newborn baby in my arms, while Matthew curled up next to me and Gilligan, our dog, lay by my feet on the floor.

Without even thinking I began to thank God; not simply for the gift of motherhood but for the endless love that filled my heart from these two precious children. Getting pregnant with our boys had not been as easy or quick as we had anticipated. Because it took longer and we had to use fertility drugs, this moment was even sweeter than I could have imagined. I suppose "a long time coming" is all relative: for many women, my journey to pregnancy would seem easy, perhaps relatively simple, but I have come to understand that life is all about perspective.

Matthew snuggled up next to me, as close as two people could be, but somehow I managed to gently pull him in even closer. As we all sat together, Matthew kept asking me when Andrew could play trains with him. I used this time to casually remind him that Baby Andrew would sleep a lot in the beginning and not be able to play with him until he got a little bigger. I smiled and told him not to worry; his new brother would be playing with him in no time. As if on cue, Andrew woke up and began to cry; he must have known we were talking about him. Matthew looked up at me, concerned, but I quickly reassured him that everything was OK; Andrew was probably just crying to tell us he was hungry. Before I knew it, Matthew had jumped off the couch and was already on his way back from the pantry with a sweet potato in his hand. He gently laid it down next to his new baby brother and said in his sweet voice that still had trouble enunciating all his letters, "Here you go, Baby Andrew."

It seems like that was just yesterday, but somehow ten weeks have already passed. Life at home with a newborn and a toddler is busy but fun. Matthew is at the age where he says the funniest things, and his personality continues to emerge more and more every day, which I love. Watching him interact with his baby brother is priceless; I can already see him being the protective big brother. He usually hollers for me to let me know Andrew is crying, as if I didn't hear him. He also likes to share his toys, and I know there will usually be a train or two in the crib when I go to get Andrew. Justin and I are both only children, so we never had the bond of a sibling ourselves. We are excited to see our two boys grow up together.

Wow, does that formula smell. I am busy cleaning Andrew up from a random yet forceful vomit. I wonder if it's his new formula, because he clearly is not sick. I run through my mommy checklist in my head one more time: *fever, rash, diarrhea?* And, thankfully, the answer to these is no. We had to make a formula switch soon after he was born, so I assume this is the case again. No big deal.

A quick sponge bath and some clean clothes, and our afternoon continues with our usual routine; Matthew playing outside while I push Andrew in the stroller. One of the things I love most about our house is how close it is to the end of a long street with a cul-de-sac, so there is little traffic. The sidewalks and driveways are lined with plenty of moms just like me talking and watching our children play. And no fun day outside would be complete without sharing popsicles and juice boxes as we fight the sweltering August heat. A pretty sweet life, if you ask me.

Fortunately, Justin and I were in agreement that two kids was the perfect number for us; it would be man-to-man defense. We generally take turns with the kids, and tonight I laugh as I listen to Matthew try and negotiate just one more book out of his daddy, while I gently rock Andrew in the room next door. I smile just thinking about how sweet Andrew is and what joy he has already brought into our family. I will admit I worried a bit: could I really love another child as much as I love Matthew? But now that question seems silly; of course the answer is yes, without a doubt. Two kids — double the love.

As Andrew lies sleeping soundly, I work quickly and quietly to finish folding his clean laundry and putting it away. However, before I can get out of his room, Andrew starts to cough and then has another huge vomit. I put down the sleeper I was folding and walk over to him. I see that not only is Andrew covered, but his crib is a mess too. Yet somehow Andrew seems completely unfazed by this and he smiles up at me as I lift my happy baby from his soiled crib and begin undressing him for his second bath in less than an hour.

Justin and I fall into bed, which seems to be our status quo ever since Andrew was born. But we are not complaining. We love our sons and know our family is finally complete, and we are so very thankful.

"Remember when we were first dating and our biggest decisions were where to go for happy hour?"

"Yeah, things have changed quite a bit from those days," Justin laughs. "Even though we might think we're still young and cool, the fact remains we have already been married for six years, and we have two kids and a dog. Not to mention there are not many hot spots out here in the burbs for happy hour, even if we had the time to go." We both laugh, something we do a lot.

On to a more serious matter: Andrew's sporadic vomiting.

"I'm not too worried at this point," I say halfway through a yawn. "It seems random. I have not yet been able to see a pattern. And the good news is he hasn't had any other symptoms of illness and clearly couldn't be happier. Hopefully we have seen the end of it, but if it continues tomorrow, I'll call the pediatrician in the morning."

"Sounds good, Honey," Justin says, as he leans over to give me a quick kiss on the forehead.

"Night, Babe, I love you," I respond. I drift off to sleep thinking about my boys; Justin, Matthew, Andrew and Gilligan, my first son, as I like to refer to him. I am the luckiest girl in the world.

During my pregnancy with Matthew, I got very sick and ended up being hospitalized. It took several days, tests and doctors to diagnose me. It was during that time that I fully realized the enormity of being a mother. I was adamant that no matter what, I would only do what was best and safe for my baby. Even though he was not born yet, my connection to him had already been made. I was his mother and from this point forward I would always do what was best for him, even if that meant sacrificing myself. I could never have imagined the bond that motherhood would bring nor could I have imagined the love it would provide. Luckily, my illness turned out to be non-life-threatening, just parvovirus. However, having it when pregnant puts the baby at risk. For the rest of my pregnancy I had to see a high risk doctor every week for several detailed tests keep a much closer eye on my baby. Matthew remained safe and did not develop any complications from the virus, but it surely took a few years off my life.

Matthew calls to me in his sweet voice, "Mommy, Baby Andrew is awake." I laugh to myself as I climb the stairs, already halfway to Andrew's room, but I love how helpful and sweet Matthew is. I enter the nursery, which I still love. It's the same as it was when Matthew was a baby. I find it calming and peaceful. The lower half of the wall is painted light blue — Bibbity Bobbity Blue if I remember correctly — while the top half is white except for the perimeter of the room, which is hand-painted to match the crib bedding: green leaves with small butterflies, little bugs and flowers. I lean into the crib, and I immediately notice a few Thomas trains in the corner.

But my eyes are very quickly brought to my smiling baby, who appears to be as yellow as a highlighter from head to toe. I grab Andrew and bring him close to me. He smiles, and Matthew is on my every step to help at the changing table. I remain calm, but I know that it is now time to call the pediatrician.

I had hoped that our plan of feeding him less formula more frequently was going to be the answer to this sporadic vomiting, but I see that we have a more serious problem going on. I immediately call our pediatrician's office and am able to schedule something almost right away. I am bummed out that our pediatrician is not in today, but I know that getting seen by any doctor is the most important thing at this point. Diapers, wipes, extra clothes, bottles, pacifier, lovie; I think that is everything for Andrew, but what about Matthew? Taking him to the doctor's office will not be fun for any of us, especially him. Luckily, my parents live nearby so I will just drop him off over there and head straight to the doctor's office. Justin is leaving work to meet us, and I am grateful he has the flexibility to do so — working for my dad has lots of perks, and this is definitely one of them. I am starting to worry; not a lot, but enough, and I need to have my best friend with me.

The pediatrician comes in the room fairly quickly and I begin to speak nervously.

"Something's wrong and it's more than just his formula." The doctor nods and calmly says he agrees. Justin and I wait patiently as he checks Andrew for all the normal basics: he listens to his heart and lungs, asking us questions all the while. Andrew is lying on the exam table with me close by to keep my hand on him, and he continues to seem happy, content and unaware that there is something wrong.

"We need to get some blood work. Clearly something is going on with Andrew's liver," says the doctor. "Here is the script for Andrew's blood work. Are you familiar with this outpatient lab? They have locations all over the city." Without missing a beat, I speak up and tell him that in the past we've gone downstairs to the lab here in the hospital.

"I want these labs done today. I am not comfortable waiting until tomorrow," I say firmly.

"OK," he says, "but I don't think your insurance will cover that."

Like I care at this point what my insurance covers or not! *My baby is yellow and has been projectile vomiting for the last several days. I couldn't care less about insurance,* I think, trying not to panic. I swallow hard to keep the tears back while Justin grabs my hand and tries to silently console me. I just don't have a good feeling.

Chapter 3

Every big problem was at one time a wee disturbance.

—Unknown

August 16, 2007

*I*t's amazing how your mind plays tricks on you. One minute I have myself so worked up I can barely think straight, but then I somehow regain my composure and talk myself back down off the ledge. I suppose the unknown is what is so tough right now. I just want the phone to ring. *Please ring. Ring, darn it.* Perhaps if I stare at it some more and continue to hold it in my hand, that will make it ring sooner. I feel like I'm back in high school trying to "will" the phone to ring, only this time it's not for something fun, like friends with plans for the night, it is actually quite the opposite.

I am waiting on the much-anticipated call from the doctor, to find out why my ten-week-old baby is yellow. Finally, after what seems like forever, although it's actually less than two hours since we left the pediatrician's office, the phone rings.

"Mrs. Akin, I have gotten Andrew's labs back, and at this point I regret that I can't tell you much other than that he is anemic and will need to have more tests done. I have called ahead to Children's to let them know you will be coming. How soon can you get there?" he asks matter-of-factly.

"What?" I say, confused. "Did you say St. Louis Children's Hospital?" *Called ahead, expecting us, need to go now, my son*: why are all these words in the same sentence? The last time I was at Children's hospital, it was for me. I was in the eighth grade getting follow-up tests done after a kidney infection. It was not fun then, and I am sure it will not be fun now.

Justin and I discuss our options and agree it will be best if he stays home with Matthew, and I take Andrew. If we ask my parents to watch Matthew then we will find ourselves trying to explain the situation, and since we don't really know much ourselves, this just seems easier. Tears blur my vision as I try to pack Andrew's diaper bag. There goes that crazy mind of mine; the fear just creeps in so quickly and quietly and then takes hold.

I pick up Matthew and give him a big hug and kiss and whisper in his ear, "I love you, Matthew." He gives me a kiss back and runs off to go play. Since we just finished eating dinner, bath and bedtime is not far off, so by the time Andrew and I get home, he should be sleeping and will have forgotten we were ever gone, or so I hope.

The hospital is not too far away, just far enough to give me time to shed plenty of tears and get my nose all clogged up. I take note of the life-size, colorful animal sculptures in front of the hospital as I pull into the massive parking garage. I come to a stop and put my window down to take my parking ticket. I realize I need to pay attention to what floor I have parked on or I will never find my car again. I look around and notice the large elephant on the wall. I make a mental note: *elephant, favorite animal at the zoo, car parked — got it.*

Gathering our things I load the stroller first and get Andrew out last; of course he is sleeping. A ride in the car is almost an automatic for that. I clip his car seat into the stroller and off we go. In the hospital we are greeted by the sound of trains running overhead, and it brings a much-needed smile to my face. Matthew loves trains, and I love watching him play trains. The lobby is brightly colored with high ceilings and I notice a hot air balloon off in the distance. *What is a hot air balloon doing in a hospital?* I wonder.

Following the exact directions from the receptionist, I push Andrew's stroller to the emergency department where I press the big round button with my elbow. The double doors open and we enter. After I give our last name, the nurse smiles and says, "We've been expecting you." *Great*, I think to myself, *this is the last place on earth that I want to be expected.* We are led into our own room. As I pass by the other rooms, I try not to look, but my fear, curiosity, and I suppose just downright confusion as to why we are here takes over. However, as I push the stroller into the room I look down at my sweet Andrew Bear and make up my mind that he is going to be fine.

One really good thing I have going for me right now is that fact that I am not squeamish around blood or needles. Spending time with my grandparents (a registered nurse and medical doctor) every summer while I was growing up exposed me to medicine at an early age, since they had their own private practice. I was my Nana's assistant, being the only grandchild. She and I were very close, and I loved learning anything and everything she would teach me.

The nurse comes in and doesn't waste a second.

"We are going to need to get an IV started so we can draw more labs. The doctor has ordered several tests; will you be OK staying in here while we get the IV started?"

"Yes, I will be staying for this and anything else that he has done" I say. "It won't gross me out, just break my heart," I reassure her. The nurse warns me that getting an IV started on babies can be difficult, and it often takes a few attempts. *Great, what am I supposed to say to that?* We end up trying both arms, feet and a wrist with no luck, and I am having a hard time staying calm. *I know he needs these labs and we have to get this IV started, but please, God, my baby should not have to be a pincushion.* As I prepare to hold Andrew still for the next attempt, all the while trying to console him, I look at the nurse and ask, "What if this one blows too?" She very calmly says, "Then we will try his head." I quickly reply, "Then it won't blow, because we are not putting an IV in my baby's head." Fortunately for Andrew, she finally gets it, and I too am grateful for this small gift. We surely need it. The nurse begins to fill vial after vial of blood — so much so I think Andrew won't have any blood left. But she seems to read my mind before I can say anything and assures me he still has plenty of blood.

Finally, I am able to cuddle Andrew in my arms and feed him some milk. He is calming down and so am I. Sitting in the vinyl chair, I keep the IV pole near us to make sure his IV doesn't get pulled while I wait patiently to find out what's next. The door slowly opens and it startles me, as I have been lost in thought with my own ideas and speculation about what is wrong with Andrew. My thoughts are interrupted with the news that we are being admitted to the general medicine floor.

"Mrs. Akin, would you like to put Andrew in a hospital crib to be wheeled up to your room or do you want to carry him?" the nurse asks.

"Admitted? What do you mean admitted?" I ask. "For what? What is going on? What is wrong with my son?" The nurse begins to talk, but I am too stunned with this news to take in what she says. All I can think is that we obviously won't be home soon like I told Matthew. I stand up and politely tell the nurse I will be putting Andrew in his stroller and pushing him myself.

I am not sure what I was expecting, but this is not it. The room is cold and sterile, and to top it off, it has another child in it. That alone leaves me shocked as we are shown to our side of the room, the A side, which I can quickly see is much smaller. I slowly sit down in the vinyl chair/pull-out bed, holding on to Andrew for dear life. The industrial metal crib sits next to us, and I shudder at the thought of putting him in there. The nurse is sweet and kind and can clearly see my fear. She begins to run through the plan for Andrew: what medicines he will be receiving, when they come in to check vital signs, etc. But I am waiting for her to finish so I can ask about the other child who is sharing our room. As she hands me linens for my chair/bed I have to ask, "Where are that little boy's parents?" She explains they are not here, she rarely sees his mom, and she only comes every few days.

"He is in and out of here all the time; we refer to him as a frequent flier. If you need me for anything just press the call button." And out she goes. What, he is alone? He has no parents with him? He is in a hospital gown and I hardly see anything that resembles something soft and familiar. He can't be more than eighteen months old. He hasn't stopped crying since we entered the room and I notice that the small TV has been positioned toward his crib with cartoons on. I suppose to entertain him? It's clearly not working; he just wants to be held and loved. I break into tears as I grasp Andrew just that much tighter. Where am I?

"Mrs. Akin? Mrs. Akin?" My eyes pop open like firecrackers; I must have dozed off. "I am a doctor from the pediatric intensive care unit (PICU) and based off Andrew's most recent labs, he is a very sick little boy and needs to be transferred to our unit." What? He is happily sleeping in my arms. *Yeah, he's still yellow, but how can he be that sick?* I think to myself. The doctor starts in about this lab value and that blood level, but I understand nothing he says. Our sweet nurse helps me by loading my purse and Andrew's diaper bag in the stroller and pushing it all down to the PICU for me. Meanwhile I hold Andrew and push the IV pole that is now connected to my son. It is all happening so fast. I look back at our roommate, who has finally fallen asleep, and shake my head as we head out the door.

As we walk down the long hall I look into the small rooms. I can barely see the children because there are so many machines. I don't know much about this unit except that it is for the sickest kids. The lights are bright and the noises are plenty, beeping sounds coming from everywhere. I unwillingly lay Andrew on the gigantic hospital bed per instructions from the doctor. The nurse is busy getting Andrew hooked up to several machines, and I ask questions about everything she is doing until I am interrupted by another doctor who asks me to step outside with him for a minute.

"Mrs. Akin, Andrew is very anemic and he needs to have a blood transfusion immediately, so I need you to sign this consent for the blood. Please read through the list of possible complications, let me know if you have any questions, and when you are done, go ahead and sign." The first sentence says that there is a one in a million chance the recipient will get AIDS, and that is as far as I get. *No way am I signing this.*

"I am more than happy to give my blood. Just let me know what I need to do."

"Sorry, but it doesn't work that way, Mrs. Akin," the doctor says with a stupid grin on his face.

"Well I am not comfortable signing this. I at least have to call my husband and discuss this." The doctor is quick to interrupt me.

"You don't understand, Mrs. Akin. Andrew has to have this blood and he needs it now." All I can think is, *you're right, I sure as hell don't understand. My ten-week-old son is in the PICU, he needs a blood transfusion, and you insist that you can't use my blood.*

I do my best to explain everything to Justin on the phone. But between my tears and the fact that I barely understand what's going on myself, it makes it very difficult to explain. However, we agree that if the doctor is insisting Andrew needs the blood then we need to sign the consent form.

"I love you, Kristin, and will be there in a second if you want."

"I know, Babe, but not yet. I'm OK. You stay with Matthew. I'll call you again when I know more."

I sign the consent, the blood gets ordered, but that is just the beginning. Not too long after my initial meeting about the blood transfusion, another doctor pulls me out into the hall to have me sign a different consent form, this time to put in a femoral line. Of course I have no idea what that is, what it means or what is going to happen, so I begin asking questions, trying to again to understand something that I really don't understand. I am struggling to even know what to ask. I feel so overwhelmed.

What I gather from my discussion with the doctor is this: Andrew is very sick, the doctors need more access into his body to give medicine, and this will help with that. The line will be more permanent than an IV and will be temporarily sewn into his groin. I am quickly beginning to understand that I am in way over my head. All I know for sure is the fact that he really needs it, so I don't even call Justin this time, I just sign. Andrew lies in the oversized hospital bed looking so tiny, so fragile, so helpless. He hasn't cried, he has no fever, no diarrhea, no rash, and he isn't even vomiting. How can he be sick enough to be in the PICU?

This room is small, white and filled with nothing but hospital equipment. The chair reminds me of a lawn chair; cream colored and made of a plastic-like material with a slight rock to it, but not for sleeping in, I have been warned. As if I could fall asleep right now, anyway. The nurses are friendly and almost conversational in tone, which shocks me, but I guess they are used to this. However, I am not. I am trying so hard to remain calm, ask questions, watch everything they do, but really I am a fish out of water in here. I feel so helpless. How can I really protect my son when I am making decisions about things I have just heard about tonight for the first time in my life?

The time goes by quickly because there is never a quiet moment in our room. There are doctors and nurses in and out constantly and I sit anxiously just watching everything happen around me. The doctor comes in with a big stack of supplies and begins organizing everything on the tray table. The nurse hands me a gown, gloves and a mask.

"You said you wanted to be present when they put the femoral line in; if so, then you need to put this all on." I nod and begin to dress in the garb I have been handed. Meanwhile, the doctor is explaining to me what she is going to do each step of the way. I watch intensely as she prepares a sterile area around Andrew's upper thigh where she will be sewing this line in. My stomach flip flops and I let out a huge sigh.

The doctor looks up at me and asks, "Are you OK, Mom? Do you need to sit down?"

"No, I'm fine," I calmly say. But I am not fine at all, really. I am watching as a perfect stranger cuts deep into my baby's thigh and begins to sew a tube into his leg. No, I am not OK with this at all and it has nothing to do with the needle and everything to do with why he needs this tube in the first place. Helplessness and fear begin to fill my throat and my breathing becomes difficult, but I force it back down and stand still, watching as she carefully finishes her stitching.

Clearly I have lost track of time. When the door opens and our pediatrician walks in, I realize it must be morning. Finally, a familiar face — I could not be happier to see him. The conversation is brief and serious.

"Kristin, do you understand what is going on? Andrew is in liver failure and has a 50% chance of making it."

Chapter 4

Children's talent to endure stems from their ignorance of alternatives.
—Maya Angelou

August 17, 2007

Justin arrives, and I practically tackle him to the ground. This is one of those moments I thank God for my amazing husband. What would I do without him? I hold on to him, and the tighter I squeeze the more tears fall from my eyes. I have never been so terrified in all my life. Luckily, Justin got to the hospital just in time for rounds with the doctors. We wait patiently, like soldiers in the army waiting for their next mission, until they reach our room. The last twenty-four hours have been a whirlwind, from Andrew waking up in his crib and being yellow to almost dying in the PICU from liver failure. It is all still very unreal.

Thankfully, Andrew is stable and Justin and I are ready for some answers, some information — some clue to what is going on with our precious ten-week-old baby. We are greeted by not one, not two, but a whole gaggle of doctors. We listen intently as they each introduce themselves and their specialty. The discussion begins, and numerous things are thrown out as possible causes of Andrew's liver failure — not one of these potential diagnoses is anything either of us has ever heard of. But more important than the diagnosis is how to treat it. How do we make my sweet Andrew better and get him out of here and back home where he belongs?

After the most intense day of my life, Andrew is finally stable enough to leave the PICU and go back to the general medicine floor, which now feels like heaven. Funny how just one day ago this room seemed so sterile and frightening, but now I welcome it. The first thing I notice is our roommate; he is still here and still alone. I fall into my vinyl chair and let out the biggest sigh of relief. I look at Andrew and just shake my head. "Son, you just took at least ten years off my life." Justin just looks at me and we begin to laugh. It feels good.

The infectious disease doctor comes in and the mood quickly changes. He is young, I am guessing about my age, but that is all we have in common, I'm sure of that. He is rigid and formal. He stands in front of

Justin and me, proudly wearing his heavily starched white doctor's coat with the crest of the hospital embroidered perfectly above his name, followed by "MD, PHD."

"At this point I am in agreement with Dr. Ritter that it appears to be a liver issue. Which is what you want, because there is a very rare immune deficiency called hemophagocytic lymphohistiocytosis, or HLH for short, but you *don't* want that, and at this point I don't think that is what it is. The thing about hemophagocytic lymphohistiocytosis is, blah, blah, blah." I look at Justin and see that he has the same look of confusion on his face. I look back to the doctor and can't help but think, *does he really think we understand any of this?* I still don't know what the first word was of the disease he just named, but he just keeps saying it. If I didn't know better I would think I just woke up in another country because I cannot understand a word he is saying. And somehow I think he knows that but doesn't really care. He's clearly impressed with his own knowledge, and his personality is about as warm and cozy as that stiff lab coat he's wearing.

Finally he finishes talking and asks if we have any questions. Of course we have questions. I quickly speak up.

"I'm sorry, but we still don't even know the name of that disease you kept throwing around, 'hemo' what, immune what? The only thing I think we understand is that we don't want it and since you don't think that is the cause of Andrew's illness, I won't waste anymore time trying to figure out what it is." Clearly, there is so much other information we are being bombarded with right now that seems to be more relevant. Besides, Dr. Ritter, the liver doctor, just walked in.

"Andrew's liver is swollen right now and it is chewing up his red blood cells: the cells that carry oxygen in your body. That is why he needed the blood transfusion yesterday. Do you understand?" We nod. Dr. Ritter's heavy Australian accent makes me feel safe for some reason, and I need that. "I think the cause of Andrew's liver problems is one of three things, but I won't know for sure until I do a needle biopsy of his liver. It is a relatively simple procedure and if you want to be in the room when I do it, you are welcome."

"Yes," I jump at that immediately, "Thank you, Dr. Ritter, I would like to be in the room. But in the meantime can you better explain the three possible causes of Andrew's liver failure?"

"Really, all you need to know at this point is that they are fixable and not life-threatening if treated properly. None of us think it is the fourth possibility, hemophagocytic lymphohistiocytosis, which is good. You don't want that. But I will know more once I do his liver biopsy and then we can talk in more detail." I let out a deep breath. Finally, some good news. Even though we remain inpatient with no mention of going home, I feel as if we are on the right path and that feels good.

"Justin, you go home. Take care of Matthew, do something fun with him this weekend. Andrew and I will be fine here, and Monday will be here before we know it. Just make sure to tell Matthew how much I love him and miss him!" Justin kisses us both goodbye and goes home. I hold Andrew in my arms with his IV pole close by and feel the tears welling up in my eyes as I tell him over and over how much I love him. He just smiles up at me and I thank God for this most brave and beautiful boy.

"Morning, Mum. We doing OK today?" I turn around to be greeted with a warm smile from Dr. Ritter, our liver doctor. "We are going to get Andrew better, and this liver biopsy will be quick and easy." I nod and smile and quietly thank him. As promised, the procedure is quick and minimally invasive. I am surprised how simple it is, relatively speaking. Andrew does great: the Benadryl has kicked in and he is sleeping, while the topical cream to numb the site has been on for plenty of time when Dr. Ritter begins. I stand perfectly still as he makes an incision on my baby's abdomen and then sticks a needle in to extract a sample of liver tissue. The procedure is quick, and before long we are back in our room. I sit back with Andrew in my arms, smiling down at him; he has no idea how proud I am of him — he truly is my hero.

I hear a light knock at our door and Dr. Ritter slowly enters. I can tell immediately from the look on his face that he has bad news.

"I'm sorry, the liver sample was not large enough and so I was unable to decipher anything from the tissue. I am going to need a larger piece."

"What does that mean?"

"Well, we will have to schedule Andrew for surgery, and he will go under general anesthesia this time so I can go in and actually cut a small wedge of his liver out. I will try and get it scheduled within the next day or so." General anesthesia, surgery, a wedge of his liver? The tears begin to fall, and I just can't help it. I want to grab Andrew and just run out of here, run as far as my legs will carry us, far away from this building. But I know there will be no running. That is merely a dream. Instead, there will be me meeting with the anesthesiologist to sign consent forms, Andrew being NPO (no milk for twelve hours before his surgery), and me worrying and waiting. I know we need to get the sample because we need to figure out what is going on, I trust Dr. Ritter and I know he would not do this if he didn't have to. But how much more does Andrew have to endure?

Another day and night pass, and Andrew and I have now been living in Children's Hospital for five days. Justin visits every day in between work and caring for Matthew. Today he is here bright and early because Andrew is having his liver surgery. He immediately notices how fussy Andrew is and asks what's been going on. I remind him that he has not had his milk for the last twelve hours and that alone seems like torture enough for a baby. We know there is not much we can do to make him happy and that breaks our hearts. Justin and I take turns holding Andrew, trying to console him, until they finally come to get us. They check Andrew's hospital wristband, grab his records from the nurse and we are transported to surgery.

Everything is so routine for everyone here, but so foreign to us. I am trying to keep myself together, but my baby is about to go under general anesthesia to have part of his liver cut out to figure out why he almost died a few days ago. There is nothing routine about that. The only solace I have is knowing Dr. Ritter will be performing the procedure, and at this point, I trust him more than anyone else. As we approach the operating room, I ask if I can come in with them for just a moment. They say yes, and I enter the freezing operating room holding my son, and ever so gently lay him down on the long, cold table.

"Mom, you might want to take off his cute pajamas and take his nice blanket with you because we will probably get blood on them."

"No, that's OK, I don't care about the blood, I just want him to have his familiar things with him."

Without anyone saying anything, we know it is time for us to go so we both lean down and kiss Andrew on the face. "Son, we love you so much and will be right here waiting for you when you're done," I quietly whisper. The nurses tell us not to worry, assuring us they will take good care of him, and I smile but think to myself, *not as good as I will.*

I am quickly coming to love this room of ours. It feels like the only safe place in this building, and when we got back here after Andrew's surgery, it almost felt like we were home — which is scary in itself. The surgery went smoothly, although it will be a while before we know anything, but the good news is Andrew came out of anesthesia well and was more than happy to be in my arms drinking his milk after the sixteen-hour hiatus.

But within minutes of getting settled back into our room I notice Andrew's belly is very swollen. Our nurse assures me it is normal to have some swelling from his procedure. However, it seems to be getting bigger and bigger before my very eyes, and Justin agrees. Feeling scared, we call for the nurse again. She listens and does her basic assessment and assures us he is fine. I swear, it is as if someone is blowing a balloon up inside his tummy right in front of us, and I don't care what anyone says, this is not normal. I press the call button again, and this time I insist a doctor come in because Andrew is now starting to cry. I can see this is getting very painful, very fast. You can cut the tension with a knife as things go from bad to worse. Our small room quickly fills with people moving around Andrew and talking amongst themselves.

Right then my parents show up. Not sure what they are witnessing but realizing it is not good, they stay outside and wait, arms wrapped around each other. Andrew's screams get louder and louder, while his belly looks like it is literally going to burst. The blue veins in his stomach are so visible they look like lines on a road map.

Justin and I are holding each other, crying, and I look at him and say, "I'm so afraid. I think he is going to die." Justin just nods and says "I know." They have ordered an X-ray, stat, but in the meantime the doctor has us sign another consent form to take Andrew back into surgery. The doctor thinks he is bleeding internally from an accidental perforation of his bowel from the liver surgery. If that is the case, we are running out of time. I cannot hold back my sobs and signing my name is almost impossible as I am shaking uncontrollably. The door has been thrown open. We are preparing to go to the operating room because we can't wait any longer. The portable X-ray machine finally shows up and takes the image of his tummy we so desperately need. The X-ray tech leaves with strict instructions to have this read immediately by the radiologist and have them call with the results. Time is ticking and Andrew continues to scream. I just know his stomach is going to burst open any second. We wait for what seems like an eternity when in reality it was only a few minutes until we receive the call from radiology with the results. Andrew is beyond miserable, and there is nothing we can do right now to help him.

The doctor comes back into our room, and I can feel the tension ease before a word is even spoken. He calmly says, "It is only gas and air left in his tummy from the liver surgery this morning. There is no internal bleeding, no need for surgery."

"What? What did you just say? Were we just seconds away from taking our son into the operating room and cutting him open when it was only gas?" Justin and I cannot believe our ears. I don't know whether to scream in anger or scream with thanksgiving. There is no doubt in my mind that that just took another five good years off my life. Justin and I smother Andrew with kisses and hugs, despite his cries. Finally, our nurse administers some medicine to help with the gas and the pain, and we let out a huge sigh.

Our two days at home have flown by, and now I'm trying to come with up with an understandable explanation for Matthew for why I am leaving my son again and taking his best friend, his baby brother Andrew with me. Gilligan looks up at me with his big brown eyes and tilts his head from side to side as if he understands as I tell him I will be back soon.

The two weeks since Andrew got sick have been a blur. How did we get here? We finally got discharged, but without any answers and with instructions to return in two days. I think the exact wording was, "Just go home and be a normal family for the weekend." Gee, that sounds good. Thanks for the advice. I am sure we won't worry about the fact that we still don't have any answers and in two days we have to check back into the hospital — the hematology/oncology floor, the cancer floor, no less.

Of course I am thankful beyond words for the fact that Andrew has been stable, that he did not need that emergency surgery and that he seems to be feeling pretty good right now. He fills my days with smiles and coos and could not be a more content baby. But I am frustrated with the doctors for sending us on this emotional roller coaster with still no answers about what initially caused Andrew's liver failure. And I am heartbroken about leaving Matthew. He is not quite three years old and doesn't understand all of this, nor should he have to. He needs his mom just as much as Andrew and having to choose is just not fair!

The elevator doors open and we step off onto Nine West, the hematology/oncology floor. I cannot believe I am here with my three-month-old son. As the tests and the meetings with doctors begin, it doesn't take long for the overwhelming fear to set in. After a few more days inpatient we finally get the news we have been praying for: Andrew does not have that rare immune deficiency, HLH. But although we are thrilled, the fact is Andrew is still sick and needs constant blood transfusions, and no one knows why.

I am getting quite good at reading the doctors' body language. Our doctor comes into the room, and before he says anything I know he has bad news. He begins to explain that Andrew needs to have a central line put in his chest. This is a surgery where a plastic tube is inserted into the chest so that the end is positioned right by the heart. The line is then sewn into the chest and the openings on the outside will allow them to draw blood, give two different medicines at the same time and give transfusions — all without sticking the patient.

"Andrew will no longer have the IV in his arm. This will be a more permanent option until we figure out what is going on."

I look at him blankly. "Do I have a choice?" I know the answer to that question before I ask. The doctor leaves and I just stand there, feeling as though I've been kicked in the gut.

The week goes from bad to worse as the tests continue to become more invasive and painful for Andrew. He gets a spinal tap and bone marrow biopsy in addition to his central line surgery. Amazingly Andrew continues to smile and seems relatively unfazed by all this mess. I wish I could be more like him.

Just when we think it couldn't get any worse, we get the news we never wanted. Some blood work was sent away to Cincinnati Children's Hospital, the experts in immune deficiencies, and the results are in. Andrew does indeed have that disease that everyone mentioned early on but thought it wasn't. Andrew has been diagnosed with hemophagocytic lymphohistiocytosis.

Chapter 5

Remember that everyone you meet is afraid of something, loves something
and has lost something.

—H. Jackson Brown, Jr.

September 2007

A bone marrow transplant is the only cure for Andrew's disease.

I keep replaying that sentence in my mind.

"Do you even know what bone marrow is?" I ask Justin.

"No, not really, but I suppose we'll learn today when we have our meeting with the doctor and the bone marrow transplant coordinator." I look at our nurse, and before I can say anything she kindly repeats her promise to stay with Andrew while we are in our meeting.

Thank God for this nurse. She is a little older than me, and I like that. Her twenty-plus years of experience is comforting right now, and comfort is something Justin and I both need. We immediately hit it off the first time we met, which just happened to be one of the worst days of my life: the day we checked into the hematology/oncology floor. It was quickly apparent we had more in common than just what was in front of us: medicine and my sick little baby. We talked about other things, normal things, and we even realized we had a mutual friend. She was an unexpected gift, and I was very thankful. Our friendly conversation was the distraction I needed before we had our meeting with Andrew's doctor.

I look at my beautiful sleeping baby. I feel a sense of calm for the moment, and I try and take in as much of that as possible as we walk out of the room. I grab Justin's hand and squeeze tight, holding on for dear life, or so it feels. I pull the heavy door shut behind us, and we begin to walk down the hall. I choke back the tears as I have already done so many times. Right now it is time for me to be focused and tears won't help at all.

We pass by several rooms and I see the same thing in each one: bald-headed and sick children. Their ages vary from teenaged to tiny babies like Andrew — discrimination does not exist here. Their IV poles nearby allow only a small amount of space between them and the toxic drugs that flow into their bodies. Some kids have pictures and artwork up that they have made with the child life department or art therapy, but in spite of those small splashes of color, it is very bleak.

"Good afternoon Mr. and Mrs. Akin. I am Dr. Howard and this is Abigail. She will be your bone marrow coordinator. Please have a seat."

The small room has two oversized black leather chairs that look like they recline, which sure don't fit in with the mismatched hospital furniture. The blinds are closed and covered with dust. I assume they stay that way so no one can see in during these meetings. *Is this the bad news room?* How many families have sat in these chairs before us getting the worst news of their lives? If the walls could talk, I can't imagine the sadness and fear they would share. I notice a rack on the wall full of pamphlets. "Living with Leukemia" is the first one, and I immediately look away.

Abigail begins by handing me a three-ring binder, telling us that this will be useful during Andrew's treatment. *What kind of treatment requires a three-ring binder?* She goes on talking. It has information about the drugs he will be receiving, a list of helpful hospital phone numbers, information about his disease and the bone marrow transplant process, a calendar to keep track of his appointments, and a special sheet for tracking his blood counts.

My heart sinks. What in the world are blood counts? But before I can ask, Dr. Howard begins to speak.

"Hemophagocytic lymphohistiocytosis is a rare immune deficiency, affecting one in every 1.2 million newborn children. There are two types of HLH: familial and infectious. Andrew has the familial type, which means he was born with it. The only cure for this disease is a successful bone marrow transplant. There is not much known about HLH because it is considered an orphan disease and receives no funding from the federal government. But make no mistake, this is not cancer."

Dr. Howard continues, "Bone marrow is the flexible tissue found in the interior of the bones. Bone marrow is also a vital element of the lymphatic system. Your bone marrow is where your red blood cells (oxygen carriers), white blood cells (infection fighters) and platelets (cells to help blood clotting) are produced."

"Do you understand?" he asks simply. Justin and I quickly nod, and he continues.

"Essentially, what we know is this: Andrew was exposed to a virus, one that we will never know, and that triggered his immune system to turn on. But after fighting the infection it was unable to turn off. Thus, it started to attack Andrew's liver, putting him into liver failure. It can affect the central nervous system and other organs as well.

"We will begin by getting blood samples from both of you and your other son to see if you are a match for Andrew. But the odds are not in your favor so just be prepared," he says, emotionless. Clearly this is not the first time he has had this conversation.

"If none of you are a match for Andrew then we will begin a formal search for a potential match on the National Marrow Donor Registry. It is an international database of people who have given a sample of their DNA. There is a very complex system that has been put in place to search all of the potential donors to find a suitable match for the recipient. There are numerous markers we look at when deciding who is the best match, if there are any at all.

"In the meantime, we will begin Andrew on the HLH protocol, which consists of chemotherapy and steroids to hopefully get the disease under control until we can transplant him."

Dr. Howard goes on for another twenty or thirty minutes, I think. I am not sure because I got stuck back on the word "chemo." I cannot get that word out of my head, and the fact that the doctor just said it so casually leaves me sick. Chemotherapy is a word he must use a hundred times a day, but in our world it is a word that has never even been uttered once. Chemo is for really sick people. It is for people fighting life-threatening illness. It is something that will almost kill you in an effort to save you, and now we are using the word chemo casually, almost conversationally, in reference to my infant son.

My brain is on overdrive with all the medical information we have just been given. My hands are sweating as I grip the three-ring binder and my stomach feels as if I just did a hundred sit ups — one big knot. *Holy cow, is this really happening? Is Andrew that sick? Will we be a match for him? Will his sweet baby hair fall out when he starts chemo?* These are just a few of the millions of thoughts that keep circling in my brain.

All of a sudden I am brought back to the room when I hear Dr. Howard say it will be a long journey, one that usually takes around two years. Two years? I am still stuck on that as he continues to explain the risks and the complications that come along with a bone marrow transplant. So much information is piling up that it's as if a box of files fell on the floor and the papers went everywhere.

I am brought back into focus as Dr. Howard says something that stands out from all the medical jargon. His voice changes a bit, and he pauses and very calmly says, "The fact is, you must try and find a balance in your family. You cannot let Andrew's disease rule your life, because you can end up sacrificing everything — your marriage, your finances, your other children — in an effort to save him, and there are no guarantees he will make it." That just took my breath away.

As promised, our nurse is still in our room when we return and without saying a word she stands up and hugs me as soon as I come in. Somehow she just knows I need that, and I begin to cry and cry and cry. They say experience is the best teacher and she is clearly an expert in helping families when they get the worst news that life has to offer. Each sob is louder than the last and she just holds me, letting the beginning of my new reality sink in.

Justin is sitting on the long, narrow bench under the big picture window, the only decent thing about our room. Well, that and the fact that we have no roommate right now, because we are a new diagnosis. They give you your own room when they first drop the bomb on you — what it takes to get a private room.

Through the blur of my tears I see that Justin is holding Andrew and I see that he, too, is crying. Finally my tears start to slow. Perhaps I am running out of them; is that possible? I gently let go of our nurse, and I see that she too has been crying. And then I hear one of my favorite sounds, the soft coos from my baby, and I look over and see that Andrew is the only one not crying. He is actually smiling.

Chapter 6

If you are truly flexible and go until ...
there is really very little you can't accomplish in your lifetime.
—Anthony Robbins

November 2007

*T*he car is finally loaded but I can barely pull myself away from the warm sun on my face as we are all together outside in the driveway. It is one of those perfect fall days; it's cool but not cold, and the trees continue to drop their last few leaves. The air is crisp and I take a huge breath. Fresh air, wow, does it feel good. I know it will be a while before I am outside with any frequency again, because it's time to check back into the hospital with Andrew.

Matthew has managed to pull every toy out of the garage in the short time it has taken us to load the car. Meanwhile, Andrew sits in his stroller watching his big brother and laughing. Our life feels normal and right, and I wish I could just freeze time. *God, please let me have more days like this,* I pray, realizing that our time on the driveway, our time as a family, all four of us at home, is such a gift.

Our time at home has been brief since Andrew first got sick. After Andrew was finally diagnosed with HLH back in September, he and I were in the hospital for another week before coming home. Luckily he was responding to treatment, so we were able to go home and do his chemotherapy through the outpatient clinic. While it made for long days, it was more than worth it to be able to go home and sleep in my own bed, play with my other son, see my husband — all the things I missed when living inpatient.

Sadly, that only lasted two weeks before Andrew's HLH flared up. He got very sick and we were admitted, and that stay lasted a month and a half. Thinking back on that time, my mind is filled with all the nightmares of having a critically ill child: long days and even longer nights; fevers and infections; a constant stream of new drugs to combat the latest complication. Waiting, lots and lots of waiting. Waiting to see doctors, waiting for lab results, waiting to see if the drugs will work, waiting to see if there was a match for a bone marrow transplant. So many tears, so much worry, so much anxiety and frustration, and so much loss of control and normality.

But something good and wonderful and special did come out of that hospital stay, and for that I am grateful. For a while Andrew's health was very touch and go, and it was then that I decided: *no matter what, I will not let this disease dictate our life.* I began to plan Andrew's baptism. I paid attention to all the details I would have normally done, just with a few minor changes. I knew that if Andrew got strong enough to have his transplant it would be months, if not years, before he could go into our church to be baptized. That would mean HLH had gotten the upper hand and I would not let that happen.

So my best friend Melissa (Mel) ordered the invitations for me, since I was stuck in the hospital, and I coordinated the ceremony with our minister and the hospital chaplain. One of the most beautiful spots in the hospital is a luscious and magnificent garden hidden on the roof. I was able to reserve it for an hour for my son's special baptism. The day came and it could not have been more perfect; the sun was shining and there was not a cloud in the sky. Our immediate family was there and our minister too. It was extra special having him, as he baptized me as an infant, married Justin and me, and baptized Matthew. Andrew looked like an angel from heaven dressed in his white baptismal outfit, and our nurse was even able to time his medicines so that he could be off his IV pole, completely free. The only thing that could have made the day better was having his big brother Matthew there. Unfortunately, Matthew was sick, but in true best friend fashion, Mel came to the rescue and took care of Matthew so our parents could come and be with Andrew. If you are lucky enough to have one best friend, you are more than lucky.

Andrew and I finally got discharged and were able to spend Thanksgiving at home. But despite having been home for almost two weeks it seems like we just left the hospital as we begin packing again to check back in for Andrew's bone marrow transplant. We start to load the kids in the car. If you didn't know better, you might think this car was college-bound, but it's not headed for anything nearly as fun or exciting. Instead our twin sheets and comforter, our new pillows, and our bags of clothes and toys from home are our necessities for life in the bone marrow unit for at least the next month. This is what we have been waiting for, working for, praying for: the day we can finally begin to heal our son of this awful disease. Despite my inner desire to just stay outside, watch Matthew play and listen to Andrew laugh, I know that is not an option.

"I know what this reminds me of," I say with a half smile, "a fishbowl." Justin laughs. The rooms in the bone marrow unit have floor to ceiling glass doors and one whole wall is glass. The room feels bigger than the rooms on the main floor, but I suppose it is because we are not sharing with someone else, thank God. It has the same big picture window as the other rooms, which I really like. It's a view to the outside world, and our room happens to overlook Forest Park, the jewel of St. Louis. It is our Central Park, only bigger. The rest of the room is white, sterile and uninviting, pretty much like every other hospital room we have been in so far. But not for long, as I have packed several things to make it our own. Matthew is very anxious to help get Baby Andrew's toys unpacked; he is always such a good helper. Watching him scamper around our room brings tears to my eyes, I will miss him so much. My heart hurts thinking about it, and the longer I stew about it the more angry I become. So I start to hang up our Christmas lights and homemade family posters. Of course, Andrew is just happy to be with his family and sits smiling at all of us.

Even though we have done it several times before, the good-byes don't get any easier. Actually, they get harder because I know that things rarely go as planned. While we hope to be in here for five or six weeks, there is no guarantee. I say it with such ease, as if five or six weeks living in the hospital is no big deal. But at this point, it really isn't a big deal because this is what Andrew must have to beat this disease, and if they said five or six months, well, I would do that too.

I know that Justin, Matthew and Gilligan are a mere thirty minutes away but living in here, it might as well be three hours. I have already missed so much time with Matthew this past fall that knowing that Andrew and I will be spending his first Christmas in the hospital is hard to swallow. But I have come to terms with this situation as best as I can. Christmas can be celebrated on any day, and that is our plan. Again, I say to this awful disease, *you will not take from me what is rightfully mine, and if I have to be flexible, then so be it!* I have no doubt it will be the best Christmas ever!

I kiss Justin — at least I will see him regularly. But it is a different story with Matthew. I lean down and begin to hug him and kiss him all over. He is laughing, and I am trying to hold back my tears. I remind him that Baby Andrew and I will be staying here for a little while so Baby Andrew can get better. I remind him of all the fun he will have with Daddy and his grandparents and with Aunt Mel, but it's really me that needs convincing. I watch Matthew give Baby Andrew what will be his last kiss until we are discharged, because from this point on, Matthew will not be allowed into this room. A smile crosses my face without my knowing as I watch my sons embrace. They have a bond that is so special and unique it is clearly the work of God.

Chapter 7

Hope is the feeling we have that the feeling we have is not permanent.
—Mignon McLaughlin

December 2007

Our time spent inpatient this past fall has been a hugely eye-opening experience for me. I quickly learned that if you want answers, or need an advocate or someone to make things happen, the answer is your nurse. Your nurse is who you spend the bulk of your day with. Nurses do so much more than just administer medicine: they know the patient's history, issues, and complications — often better than the doctors. I have come to know the nurses quite well and have formed a bond with several of them.

I am so very thankful for these women. They have stepped into my life in the darkest of hours and helped me through the most difficult times, which I know is not part of their job description. I can't imagine not having them and I look forward to seeing them, knowing their unique personalities are what make my days brighter. Like most children's hospitals, this is a teaching hospital, and that makes your primary nurse all the more important. There are always new medical students and residents on the floor. They do a short rotation and move on, which makes it impossible for them to know the patients' individual complications and disease processes very well.

I hear the door slide open and know without looking it's our nurse. The pump just started to beep, letting us know this medicine is done. I reach up to silence it, something I have done a million times already. The nurse and I start to chat while I am still lying in bed, next to Andrew as he sleeps. I know it is just a matter of seconds before he wakes and our day begins as she gets the blood pressure cuff to take his morning set of vitals.

"We were sleeping so soundly, for once," I say. "I really did a good job on our bed this time, between the egg crate padding, the new T-shirt sheets and our queen-sized comforter from home. This bed is so snuggly." Our nurse just laughs. How I wish I could just pull the covers over our heads and tell her to go away, maybe put the "do not disturb" sign on the door. But this is far from a hotel, and she is not a housekeeper, and it doesn't work like that. I get out of bed, careful not to get tangled up in Andrew's lines. Standing in my nightgown and slippers, I flip to the yellow tab in my binder for our calendar and refresh my memory of our upcoming week: surgery today, chemo for the next six days, two days of rest and then the bone marrow transplant. I read out loud, and our nurse nods in agreement. Surprisingly, I am relatively calm; living in the hospital for most of the last three months has been a crash course in hematology, HLH, bone marrow transplants, and lots of other medical tests, drugs and procedures I never wanted to know about.

I make a mental note to update our CarePage later today. Soon after Andrew was diagnosed, a friend told me about this free website that the hospital offered as a way to update family and friends during your child's illness. I can't imagine what I would have done without it. Justin and I were overwhelmed trying to return calls and e-mails from everyone, but this took care of that. It has also been a great support system; people can leave comments for us to read and those are often the only positive things I hear all day. I have been amazed at the outpouring of love and encouragement from friends and strangers alike. I try to update frequently and post new pictures to give people a glimpse into our lives. But honestly, no matter what I write, no one can begin to understand what it is really like to live in a hospital, fighting for your child's life. Our CarePage is more than just updating about Andrew, it is a reminder to everyone at home to be thankful for what you have. In an instant, your life can change too, so don't sweat the small stuff.

Staring up at the Christmas lights that line the perimeter of our room, my eyes well up with tears when I think about everything that has transpired since that life-changing day in August when Andrew first got sick. They begin to fall quickly, wetting my face and neck, but I keep quiet because I don't want to wake my sweet sleeping baby next to me. We are in our normal position: me on my side with Andrew right next to me and his lines loosely lying over my waist as they run up to the IV pole next to our bed. Our heads are touching on the pillow and the blankets are up near his chest, near my arm so as not to cover his face. Moments like this I just can't believe he is so sick, that his life lies in the balance. But then I think back over all Andrew has had to endure: a liver biopsy, liver surgery, a femoral line, eight blood transfusions, twenty doses of chemo, one EKG, multiple X-rays, three bone marrow biopsies, lumbar punctures, a hearing test, a vision test, a dental exam, a GFR, a PFT and two central lines. How many times has he been stuck with needles, endured fevers, fought infections and cried for hours in pain? Yet I think the morning soon after he had begun chemo when we woke up with his hair all over our pillow was among the worst, at least for me.

We have lived in complete isolation from everyone since Andrew was diagnosed, and Justin and I could probably use treatment for our new obsessive-compulsive disorder with germs. While Andrew was at home we would wash our hands so many times a day they bled, strip down to our underwear whenever we came home from being out and go straight to the shower, and wash everything that could fit in the washer or dishwasher repeatedly. There was a can of Lysol and hospital grade wipes in every corner in our house, car and diaper bag. Of course Andrew went nowhere other than the hospital; no one could come near him. It was a battle every day for us to stay healthy to try and protect Andrew. But now all of that is behind us because we are hours away from Andrew receiving his lifesaving cells. I dry my tears and begin to smile as I let go of all of that sadness and pain and replay the amazing event that happened today.

Earlier in the afternoon, I met with the relaxation therapist. She had been coming to our floor for the last several weeks to help families with stress relief and relaxation techniques. She is a very neat woman—very different in a lot of ways, but I think that is part of what I am drawn to. When I asked her about her religious background she talked about her traditional upbringing but her now more spiritual beliefs. She focuses a lot on energy and intention, and our sessions are usually spent working on breathing exercises and basic meditation techniques. Before meeting her I had no experience with these kinds of techniques, but I have been keeping any open mind and am starting to really enjoy it.

But today was very different, and a good kind of different; something I won't forget for a long time. The session started out like our earlier ones, with me lying down on a blanket on the floor in the BMT parent lounge. The lights were off and there was instrumental music playing quietly in the background. Before starting, she asked if she could touch my head if she washed her hands. Clearly my germ phobia is public knowledge. I smiled and said yes. I barely felt her hands on my head, yet I started to feel an immense amount of heat. It felt like something strong, but I'm not sure what it was, or even how to describe it. She continued with our session, and neither of us said a word.

On finishing, she shared the following: "I hope you don't think this is weird, but during this session you were surrounded by angels, and they wanted me to tell you that they are here with you." I would be lying if I didn't say I was caught off guard by this. I wasn't sure what to say but took it at face value and said, "Thank you." This was certainly something new to me, outside the realm of my traditional Presbyterian upbringing — but something I respected nonetheless. I was anxious to call Justin and tell him about it, but before I got the chance, our nurse came in with a gift for Andrew: a balloon and a ceramic angel that said "believe" on it. The gift came from the very first nurse we had when Andrew first got admitted to Children's. She continues to follow our story on CarePages.

Not long after that I was doing my daily room cleaning, and as I moved a small stack of cards to wipe down the counter, something fell out onto the floor. Bending down to pick it up, I began to smile. It was a necklace with a cross on it and the card that it was wrapped around said it was called a guardian angel. It was a small cross on a black string, and the card said to wear it until it wore off. Then, to top off the day, our night nurse came in and what did she have on her scrub top? What else but angels? I commented on the angels, and she said she wanted to wear something special tonight for Andrew, since this is the eve of his transplant. Wow. At that point I realized that what the relaxation therapist said today was real. God is listening. He is watching, and He uses people, places and things to help us know He is with us. We just have to be receptive. Despite all my time in church growing up, I learned a lesson in faith today that I would never have heard sitting in a pew. It was a clear reminder that we don't always get what we want, but we always get what we need. I could not be going to bed any happier than right now. Andrew and I have been blessed with angels, and that is exactly what we need!

All along we had hoped Andrew would be receiving bone marrow since that is what the doctors said they would prefer, but as suspected, neither I nor Justin nor Matthew is a match for Andrew. The initial search on the bone marrow registry did not reveal any significant match for Andrew, and time was growing short. Andrew's HLH had begun to flare up, and he was becoming increasingly sick. Going with umbilical cord cells was our only option. When I had my boys I only knew about banking the cord blood to save in case your own baby got sick, which we did not do. It would not have worked in this case anyway. I did not know you could donate the cord cells for free. What a waste, to think so many cord cells are thrown away when they could go to the cord bank and be used to save someone's life.

"Can you believe Andrew is having his bone marrow transplant today?" I ask Justin.

"No, it feels very surreal." I agree completely. With my camera in hand, I run out of our room when I see the woman from the lab with our cells. She is carrying a small red cooler — Igloo I believe — and I begin snapping pictures like the paparazzi. She, of course, is laughing at me as I ask to take a picture of her holding the cooler. I must document everything; this is very baby book-worthy. I grab my phone when I see it is my parents calling.

"Do you have a few minutes?" they ask. "We're just so anxious and have a few more questions." I begin my standard speech without much thought.

"Having a bone marrow transplant is a very complicated procedure," I remind my parents. "Andrew will stay in our room and will be hooked up to a heart, oxygen and pulse monitor and will have his blood pressure and temperature taken very frequently. The nurse and doctor will be the only ones in the room with us. The actual receiving of the cells is very anticlimactic. There's no surgery or anesthesia; they will simply push the cells into Andrew's body through his central line via a syringe. He will be awake and I will get to hold him the entire time. It probably won't take too long, since he is little and won't be getting that many cells.

"Our nurse warned us that the cells have a preservative in them that most people think smells a lot like creamed corn, and Andrew will smell like it for at least twenty-four hours. His breath, his skin, everything will emit that smell, but other than that it should be quick and simple. He has already gotten some medications to help with possible reactions, and that is why he will remain on the monitors for twenty-four hours, to keep any extra close eye on him."

"And when do we find out if it worked?" my dad asks.

"Yeah, that's the hard part of this process. Our doctor said it will be at least two to three weeks before we see any counts come in, and then we won't know what his engraftment is until they do a bone marrow biopsy at thirty days post transplant. It takes time for the new cells to move in and set up shop, so to speak. During the next few weeks Andrew will be dependent on red blood cell and platelet transfusions until his new cells start to work. He has zero immune system to fight off any infection, so even bugs from his own body are a major risk right now. Getting the cells is actually the easiest part of this entire process."

"Kristin, we could not be more proud of you. You sound like a doctor, and we just don't know how you are doing it," my mom says.

"Mom, I am far from a doctor and besides, what are my options? Andrew is my son, I love him with all my heart and I will not stop until he is well and home with us where he belongs. Listen, I have to go. They're coming into our room right now. I'll call you later, I love you both."

Our nurse is busy hooking Andrew up to all of the different monitors, which he will need to keep on for the next twenty-four hours, she reminds me. I take a few more pictures and try to comprehend what is about to happen. Our nurse practitioner walks into our room holding a gigantic plastic syringe — the biggest one I have ever seen — filled with what looks like blood but is actually cord cells.

"That's it?" I ask, and she smiles. "Yes, that's it." It is Tuesday, December 7, 2007, at 10:06 a.m., when our nurse begins pushing the cells from the oversized syringe into Andrew's central line. At 10:18 a.m. she is done. I am in awe of what just happened, and when I look at Justin I see his tears match mine; tears of joy, for once. A perfect stranger somewhere on this planet decided to donate her baby's cord blood and today her baby's cord cells have given my baby a second chance at life. Don't ever underestimate the power of an anonymous gift — it might just be the life-saving answer someone is looking for.

Transplant day is over, and now we must patiently wait for the new cells to move into Andrew's bone marrow and start working. Did I say patiently? The chemo he received last week was to destroy part of his bone marrow to make room for the new cells to move in. But until that happens, Andrew has no immune system at all, which is why we are living in complete isolation. We are constantly reminded that one of the biggest risks for bone marrow transplant patients is the risk of infection in the weeks and months after the transplant.

I start every day with the same routine. I wipe down our bed, our doors, the light switches, the drawers that contain our medical supplies, and everything else I can get my hands on. The wipes I use are hospital grade and the label says they kill everything from the common flu to HIV-1. We even have a double set of doors on our room. If one door opens before the other door closes, an alarm will sound. There is a special HEPA air filtration system as well. We never forget why we are here, living in isolation, away from everyone and everything. It truly is a matter of life and death.

Our nurse begins to go through Andrew's schedule for the day; what medicines when, etc. It is very familiar and I almost anticipate her next words until she mentions something new. Beginning today, which is day +1 post transplant, Andrew will be on fluid restriction until he begins to engraft.

"We use a basic formula to determine how much fluid he will be allowed every twenty-four hour period. We have to account for his oral and IV medicines as well, so unfortunately that does not leave very much for him to actually take by mouth."

I stare at the nurse and sputter, "What? What did you just say? You know he normally takes six ounces of milk every four to five hours with the exception of nighttime and now he can only have eight ounces every twenty-four hours?! How am I going to keep him happy? Are you kidding me? This is insane!"

"I know," our nurse says, "This will be challenging, but keep in mind he can have as much food as he wants."

Well, that's great, because he has never had solid food in his life, so I am sure once I explain the situation to him, he will start eating today. I am so frustrated right now I don't know what to do.

Before I can get another word in our nurse adds, "Andrew will also be starting two additional oral medications today, in addition to his mouth care. He must get mouth care four times a day. You will scrub his mouth and tongue with this disposable sponge to help prevent mouth sores, which is a side effect of the chemo." She looks at me and asks, "Do you have any questions?"

I very calmly say, "No. Please just give me a few minutes alone with Andrew." She walks out, and I pull the curtain across the glass doors, closing off the view into our fishbowl for the time being. Andrew has always been a big milk drinker and it seems to bring him more comfort than normal. Now even that is being taken away. I feel so helpless. I have almost no control over anything anymore. Everything is dictated to us. The list of rules living in the bone marrow unit is a mile long. And I really don't mind, because I know it is for the safety of my son and the other children in here — yet, as the days pass, I feel more and more like a prisoner although we didn't do anything to deserve punishment. I am frustrated — not at anyone — just this situation. I hate HLH; I hate everything about it and what it has done to my family, especially my son Andrew. I begin to pace. *This is not going to work,* I repeat. *I have to figure something out; I will figure something out.*

As the saying goes, necessity is the mother of invention. I could not be happier right now. After I got over the initial shock of the fluid restriction and the fact that Andrew turned up his nose at every food I put in front of him, I realized something had to be done. I can't expect my six-month-old son to just start eating mashed potatoes today when he has never had them or any other food before. Andrew has been sick since he was ten weeks old and hitting the normal milestones had not been our priority. Weeks went by where he was so sick we could barely get him to drink his milk, let alone try out solid food. He loves his milk, his bottles and his special nipples, so what if I put something in the bottle that he could still drink but wasn't milk? All of a sudden I was like a mad scientist. I got a jar of applesauce and poured that into the bottle. I gave it to Andrew and waited, and within seconds he was drinking it down. Before I knew it, he had finished off the whole bottle, one jar of applesauce. The nurse had said he could have as much food as he wanted each and every day, so this was the answer — baby food in the bottle.

Andrew seemed to like the baby food; I stuck to fruits and he tolerated them fine. I think a big part of it was being able to drink it from his bottle. He was extremely attached to his bottle, so with his milk intake so limited, this did the trick until the fluid restriction was lifted. I had figured out how to beat HLH once again and that made me happy. I know that in the end I have little control over the final outcome, but whatever I can do every day to make Andrew happy and comfortable, and to make his life as normal as possible, then I am going to do it. That's my job; I am his mom.

Christmas has come early: the news we have been waiting for, praying for, hoping for, has finally come. It is day +13, which just happens to be my lucky number, and Andrew is starting to engraft. Hooray! The new cells are working. Justin and I are overjoyed, and our doctor is pleasantly surprised at how well Andrew is doing and how quickly he is starting to engraft. The big D-word has been thrown around (discharge), and that is always a great sign. It probably won't be before Christmas, but who cares? As long as things continue to go well, we will celebrate when we get home, whatever day that might be. Besides, Christmas isn't about trees and presents, or cookies and lights; it is about family being together, it's about love. And we have already been given the best gift ever: a second chance at life for our son.

December 26, 2007: Andrew and I are home after being in the bone marrow unit for thirty days. It is difficult to describe how it feels to be here. It is simply perfect. Being together under one roof is a gift that keeps on giving. However, it is a huge responsibility. While we have grown accustomed to the daily care that is required for his central line, he is now on so many oral medicines every day in addition to several IV medicines that we have to administer. Just doing the weekly central line dressing change is a big deal. It has been an adjustment, but we are more than willing to carry the weight of this job to keep him here with us.

Besides, there is nothing better than to see Matthew interact with Andrew. It's as if no time has passed at all. I am blown away by the unconditional love I see between these two boys. There is no jealousy on Matthew's part, and they both seem to pick up and move on, not letting this disease get in the way of anything. My children are teaching me lessons daily. I am in awe and so honored to be their mother.

Justin and I continue to be a tad anxious about Andrew's continuing engraftment. We won't know his progress until day +30 when he has a bone marrow biopsy. We have no reason to think his engraftment will be anything but 100% but we will feel better once we see the actual results. We remain cautiously optimistic that 2008 will bring good news and a new chapter in Andrew's illness: the beginning of his recovery.

In the meantime, our time at home is busy. Life does not stop when you have a sick child, which sometimes can be good. Justin still goes to work, Matthew wants to run and play from sunup till sundown and Gilligan barks at everyone who walks by. Not to mention, Andrew and I still have to visit the hospital quite a bit for lab draws and check-ups. But this all feels pretty normal, all things considered, and we love it. To be honest, I am not sure who is happier with me being home, me or Matthew. We missed each other so much and I know Justin loves having us both home as well. Just taking Matthew to nursery school and being able to pick him up is wonderful; I love it and so does Andrew. Once Matthew gets in the car, Andrew goes crazy, laughing and smiling.

Today started like most other days in the outpatient clinic, until our social worker, bone marrow coordinator and doctor walk into our small, cramped room. I knew right away something was not good — you never get the social worker when something good happens — but for the life of me, I had no idea what they were going to say.

"I am so sorry, Kristin, but Andrew is only 20% engrafted," our bone marrow coordinator says. *What? I don't remember the doctor ever talking about this. No one told us this could happen. This was not on the mile-long list of possible complications. I just don't understand.* Everyone walks out of the room for the moment. They know we need a few minutes alone. Justin and I look at each other, completely stunned. I begin to cry, and Justin pulls me up so he can hug me.

"I know Babe, I don't understand either," he says through his tears. Time stands still as we hold each other and cry for a while.

I hear the door slide open and our doctor walks back in. I manage to wipe my tears away, sit down, and ask point blank: "Now what?"

Chapter 8

We must embrace pain and burn it as fuel for our journey.
—Kenji Miyazawa

February 2008

*D*espite the joy of being home, my mind continues to swirl with the devastating news: only 20% engrafted. I just never knew that could happen. But then why would I? I never even knew what bone marrow was until five months ago. The more I learn, the more I realize there is to learn. The immune system — what an amazing yet complicated system. In my mind I replay the list of possible complications during transplant: infection, veno-occlusive disease, graft-versus-host disease; but I don't remember reading about partial engraftment. There has been so much to learn from the beginning. I am constantly trying to research and learn as much as I can. I know it is my job to be Andrew's advocate and to do that I need to understand his disease, its treatment and its risks. While I am sure that partial engraftment was discussed somewhere, I just don't remember it.

Even if I did, what difference would it make now? *What went wrong? Why did he not fully engraft? Does Andrew not deserve to get better? Hasn't he endured enough? Hasn't our family endured enough? God, I feel like you are pushing me past what is fair, what I am capable of — past what is more than reasonable.* The tears fill my eyes, and no matter how many times I replay this conversation in my head, I am not getting any answers. I am angry: quite frankly, pissed off. Maybe we were overconfident since Andrew got out of the bone marrow unit so quickly? Was it because he never had a high a fever or had any life-threatening complications during the first weeks following his transplant?

He seemed to sail through, his happy disposition often making me forget, for just a moment, that he was battling for his life. But the fact remains that Andrew has been sick since he was ten weeks old, he has spent most of his life at St. Louis Children's Hospital. He has been through more than most will experience in a lifetime, doesn't he deserve to get better?

Justin comes and sits down next to me ever so quietly and puts his arm around me.

"Honey, I too am devastated and angry and confused. But I do know we both love our boys more than anything, and we will do everything in our power to protect them. So now we must dig deep, deeper than before and start again."

"I know," I say through my tears. "I just need to have a pity party for a little bit." I laugh a little. We smile at each other, and I hold him tightly until the sound of Andrew's beeping pump interrupts us.

These times together, just the two of us, allow me to let my guard down. I try not to cry in front of the boys, or in the hospital. I try to keep it together for the most part. It's only in the car, in the shower, and when I'm alone with Justin that I can let it out.

It is hard to believe, but we have actually gone an entire month without being inpatient. Andrew has been doing very well, despite his low engraftment. The time at home is such a gift and we have been treasuring every moment. We are really starting to see Andrew's personality emerge. He is sweet and joyful, but most of all, happier than any baby I have ever known. As far as his health, he remains stable. We still spend quite a bit of time in the clinic each week, but outpatient is always better than inpatient.

Spending so much time in the hospital has exposed me to an entirely new culture, one that I knew very little about before Andrew's illness. Hospitals have their own language, their own rules and regulations, even their own cops. They have their own points of pride and their own struggles as well. Unfortunately, they have to deal with much more than just sick children. They also have to deal with neglectful parents.

I have seen it time and time again: children dropped in the clinic to receive their chemo or radiation alone, children admitted to the floor and not a family member to be seen for days. Family members who are more concerned with getting their free meal tickets and prepaid phone cards than their child's condition and survival outcome. And there are the children who always seem to get admitted right before the holidays, and for the exact reason you think: to get free stuff. It is downright disturbing. Being a parent of a critically ill child is hard. It is overwhelming, it is terrifying, and it puts strains on your family and life in so many different ways. It is just not fair, but they are still our children and it is our responsibility to care for, love and protect them.

But if that was not enough to make you want to run and hide, there is the inevitable: death. Not every child who enters this building will leave. Some will die. Many die. Everyone knows someone who has died, but most people don't know a child who has died and thankfully are not surrounded by death, day in and day out. For me, that is without a doubt the hardest part of living in the hospital.

Before Andrew got sick I never spent much time thinking about children dying. Now I can't stop thinking about it, not just the uncertainty about my own son, but about the other kids we have gotten to know. I knew it was only a matter of time, but nothing could have prepared me for the first one.

Larissa, a little girl who was fighting cancer, was one of the first kids we met when we moved onto the floor. She was about six or seven years old, sweet and friendly, and beautiful, despite being bald. She loved babies, and whenever she was feeling well enough to leave her room, she stopped by to wave and see Andrew. Her mom and dad were soft-spoken, loving, dedicated, and of course scared to death like most of us here. I specifically remember this past Halloween, as we spent it inpatient, as did she.

Andrew dressed up as a pea in a pod. This costume was beyond cute: a bright green bunting sack with big, round peas attached to the front with Velcro and a little green hat that was supposed to be the stem. I don't know what was puffier, his steroid-laden cheeks or his puffy little body in the bunting. Either way it was adorable! Justin and I had switched places so I could go home to trick-or-treat with Matthew and his friends, but sadly that did not happen. I had been looking forward to having some one-on-one time with Matthew for weeks, since Andrew and I had been inpatient for some time. I was so excited to just be with him, make his dinner, read him books, let him sleep with me and snuggle; just be his mom. Being away from Matthew broke my heart, and I will never stop missing the time I didn't get to spend with him. This is one of the most difficult things about having a critically ill child: the other siblings pay a price and it's not their fault.

Matthew was running a fever and vomiting that day, clearly not trick-or-treat-bound. I quickly gave all of our candy to a neighbor to hand out and turned off our porch light. Disappointment: an emotion I had become very familiar with lately. We both needed this fun night together and somehow sickness reared its ugly head again. After some Tylenol and a warm bath, Matthew seemed to be feeling a little better, enough to try a little mac and cheese for me, which made me feel a little better. I tucked

Matthew into our bed on my side, his residence whenever I am inpatient with Andrew, and I crawled into Justin's side. We lay next to each other, so close I could smell his lavender lotion, my favorite. Before I had even finished our first book he was fast asleep.

"I'm sorry Matthew," I whispered. "I am so very sorry. I am sorry I have been absent for so long, I am sorry your baby brother has been so sick, I am sorry about every minute I have missed with you, and I will spend the rest of my life trying to make it up to you." Ever so slowly and quietly I got out of bed and went downstairs to the kitchen to whip up some cupcakes to take back with me to the hospital later tonight.

Halloween in the hospital is not quite the fun it is on the outside world, especially for the kids on our floor. If they are feeling well enough to get out of bed and their blood counts are high enough, then they are able to trick-or-treat. There is an administrative floor in the hospital that turns into the main trick-or-treating area. People from all the different departments come there to hand out candy and see the kids. Because the children on our floor had compromised immune systems, they let our kids go first. As for the kids that can't leave the floor: they just go from room to room.

I had made Halloween cupcakes to hand out, since I knew we would have some trick-or-treaters at our door. Larissa stopped by our room and had a teething ring for Andrew because she knew he couldn't eat candy. I was so touched. In spite of her own illness, she was thinking of others. So when the day finally came, despite the fact that we had all known she was getting worse, I was in utter shock. I will never forget Larissa or the impact her death made on me. She was a fighter. She gave it all she had and I admire her courage. I know she is not forgotten, in my heart and many others as well. Her parents and I had shared our stories, and our fears and hopes for our children. Seeing them leave the floor for the last time broke a piece of my heart and left me feeling scared to death.

After we received the news about Andrew being only 20% engrafted, our doctor made changes to his immune suppression drugs to hopefully allow more of his donor cells to take over and increase his engraftment. Now it's time to see if the changes we made did what he hoped for. It has been a month since his first engraftment; maybe time has worked in our favor. We head to the hospital for his bone marrow biopsy. At this point I know the drill — this is Andrew's fourth one. I sign the consents and listen as the anesthesiologist reviews the list of possible complications, with death rounding off the list. I am not too concerned about death from the procedure, but I am worried about his engraftment numbers. *Please let it be above 50%. Please, God let it have gone up.*

Luckily the procedure does not take too long and soon I am back with my baby in the recovery room. It's fortunate that he tolerates anesthesia so well, because he has undergone it more times than I can count offhand. I look at him while I wait for him to wake. I am not any more OK with the lines running from his tiny body today than I was the day they went in. Andrew begins to stir. His eyes open and he sees me, and I know he is ready for his milk. It has been over twelve hours since he had any and being fed will make him more happy than anything else. The nurse takes one more set of vitals and unhooks him from the monitors, and I begin to get him dressed. She reviews the instructions for how to care for the biopsy site; this, too, I know. I have learned quite a bit over the last six months. Andrew's care has gotten more complex, and more responsibility continues to fall on us, but we are more than happy to help any way we can. This little bit of control helps us cope with a mostly uncontrollable situation.

"Honestly, it seemed relatively simple. Well, maybe 'simple' isn't the word," I say, "but having the hundred-day schedule made it seem doable." Get chemo; have transplant; check engraftment; and wean immune suppression drugs, being off everything by day +100. Day +100 seemed like the magic day; get there and you are good to go. But now I know that timeline was the "in a perfect world" scenario. Justin and I sit, waiting patiently for what we hope will be great news, but when our doctor walks in I immediately get a bad feeling.

"There are several different types of cells that we look at in the bone marrow biopsy, as each one plays a different role in beating the disease. We know that while it is not important to have 100% of all cell types, it is necessary to have at least 50% of certain cells to keep HLH away. I am sorry to tell you this, but the cells Andrew really needs to beat HLH actually went down to 0%. The other cell group went down to 8%," our doctor explains. "It is not looking very good, despite our best efforts with the manipulation of his immune suppression drugs. But we still want to have some additional blood work done, and that has to be sent off to Cincinnati Children's Hospital."

We stare straight ahead for a while, speechless.

"So what does this mean?" I finally say.

"I think Andrew is going to need another bone marrow transplant. I will confirm that when the labs come back."

Chapter 9

I know God will not give me anything I can't handle.
I just wish that He didn't trust me so much.

—Mother Teresa

Spring 2008

I suppose the saying is somewhat right. Time does heal: not all wounds, but it surely helps. It took some time to get over the initial shock that Andrew's bone marrow transplant had failed and he would need another one. Talking about it with friends and family, trying to explain over and over again why it didn't work and what we are going to do differently — I think that was actually helpful, too. I found myself feeling stronger, more confident, positive it would work this time.

"But how are you going to do it? Just start back from the beginning with all the tests beforehand, all the chemo, all the weeks away from Matthew?" my friend asks me. "I couldn't do it; I couldn't handle it. I don't think I could go back in there and do it all again," she says.

I couldn't help but laugh, sort of. "What is my option? Tell the doctors we're not interested in saving our son's life? That it's all just too much to do again so we'll just stay home and wait until he dies?"

"Kristin," she stammers. "What . . . is that what you just inferred? But don't say he's going to die," she says, looking at me very seriously.

"You know what, he will die for sure if we don't do this second transplant, and even if we do, he still might die. This is something I think about and have not stopped thinking about since he first got diagnosed. I am not being negative or morbid, just facing the reality of our situation."

"I'm sorry, I didn't mean to upset you."

"You didn't upset me; HLH upsets me, and that's just the way it is. But the love I have in my heart for my children is endless and nothing will keep me from doing everything I can for them. You would do the same. When your back is against the wall, it is amazing how you find strength, energy and hope you never knew you had. Besides, I don't expect you to get it. You have to live it, and I hope you never do."

I always look forward to dinnertime when we are home from the hospital, because that means Justin will be home from work. I could not have chosen a more loving and caring husband. From the minute he walks in, he is all hands on deck; happy to help with the boys from feeding to baths. He is my best friend and partner. We have been happily married for six years, and dealing with a critically ill child, a situation that causes many couples to struggle or even divorce, has made us more committed to each other and our family than ever.

From the minute he walks in I can tell he has something to tell me.

"Babe, I won a national sales contest!" I stop chopping vegetables and turn around, waiting to hear more. With a huge smile on his face, Justin proudly tells me he won an all-expense-paid trip to Disney World. Gosh, that is completely unexpected but so very needed! I am not sure who is more excited right now, Justin or me. He pulls out the brochure and we start flipping through the pages together. The pages are colorful and full of life, making everything from eating breakfast to walking through the lobby look fun. We are both getting so excited about how much fun would it be to take Matthew to Disney World, together.

But we know that's impossible right now. I need to stay home with Andrew, and that's OK. I realize that these disappointments are minimal and short-lived. Disney World isn't going anywhere and it will be all the sweeter when we can all go together as a family. And for all the heartache that HLH has brought our family, it has given some gifts that I would never trade. Andrew and I have had so much one-on-one time. Even though his development has been delayed and he is still very much like an infant, that gives me the chance to hold him more, feed him, care for him, and with another transplant looming, I treasure every minute with him, because the future is not guaranteed.

Despite our circumstances we still want Matthew to have as normal a life as possible.

"Justin, I want you to take Matthew. I know he will have the time of his life and he deserves to go."

"I agree with you, Kristin, but you deserve to go just as much as I do. Besides, Matthew needs to have his mommy and his daddy. Now, before you say no, just hear me out. Andrew has been doing really well lately. Starting him back on the HLH protocol has made a big difference and his disease is quiet right now. Things are moving along, they have begun the search for a new donor, his tests are being scheduled, there is nothing more we should or could be doing to prepare for his second transplant. So, I was thinking we could have one of his primary nurses come and stay with him at the house so you can come too. It will only be a few days, and who can care for Andrew better than one of his nurses?"

"What, leave Andrew? I don't know, I really need to think about it. It's not a matter of trusting his nurses, I've just never left him. I would be so far away. But the thought of you, me and Matthew at Disney World is very tempting. Let me sleep on it."

I should have known better. I have everything packed, I've typed up pages and pages of notes for our nurse, but as I am hooking Andrew up to his last medicine of the night, I can feel he has a fever. I know it without taking his temperature, but I do anyway. One hundred and two point four — that buys us an automatic minimum twenty-four-hour admission to Children's Hospital. We begin to do what we have done so many times before. Justin starts packing Andrew's things so I can grab my things. As we load the car, we are quiet because there is nothing to say. We both feel the same way: sad, disappointed, angry, overwhelmed — just tired of it all. Finally, I speak up.

"Matthew still deserves to go. He shouldn't be punished because his brother is sick. You two go and have fun." We hug each other and I run up to kiss Matthew again since I won't see him again for several days as he heads to Disney World and we head back to the hospital.

Justin and Matthew make it to Disney World as planned while Andrew and I spend the night in the hospital, as not planned. We are getting ready for bed when the door opens and the resident sticks his head in to tell me all of Andrew's tests were negative, and since he looks so good, we will probably be getting discharged tomorrow morning, right past the twenty-four-hour mark. I am relieved to hear the news and can't help but laugh to myself, thinking that Andrew got this fever because he heard I was going to leave him to go to Disney World with his brother. Justin and I are cautiously optimistic and decide that it is still worth trying to make it to Disney World. Better later than never. I get into bed with Andrew and fall asleep, happily knowing that we are going to be getting discharged tomorrow and I am still Disney bound.

Andrew and I wake up early, as usual. It's not like we have a choice with all the people going in and out of our room. Our nurse comes in.

"I'm sorry, Mom, but the lab just called, and they said something has started to grow from the cultures we drew yesterday when Andrew was admitted. It is from his red line, and they know it is a gram-negative bug."

"I know: something from inside his own body."

"Yes, you're right. The final identification has not come back yet, but they feel strongly it is it pseudomonas. Luckily, the antibiotics that they started Andrew on yesterday when you got admitted for his fever should cover it."

"OK, so what does this mean? I am assuming we are no longer getting discharged today? I guess I should cancel my flight to Disney World.

"What if it's not pseudomonas? What if we don't have the correct antibiotic? What if he spikes another fever?" I could just scream. "Why can't anything go right just for once? Don't my kids deserve a break? Why must we always have to choose between one or the other? Why does trying to save one's life hurt the other one so much?" I finally stop my ranting and look at our nurse.

"I'm sorry," is all I can muster. Our poor nurse, what do I really expect her to say? "Thanks for listening. Sometimes I just feel we can't win for losing, you know?"

"It's OK. I don't understand, but I do understand that this sucks and I don't know how any of you parents do it. To answer your question, you are still getting discharged. And for what it's worth, I think you should still try and go to Disney World." I finally smile and say, "OK, then go get our discharge papers, please, 'cause I am going to Disney World today!"

I have just enough time to get us home and settled before our nurse, Lauren, comes over and I am out the door on my way to the airport. It's hectic but that's probably a good thing — it means I don't have time to change my mind. I make it to Orlando and walk into the hotel room, and surprising Matthew is better than I could ever have imagined. He is beyond excited to see his mommy, but not half as excited as I am to see him. He had been asleep and I have to assure him he is not dreaming. I shower quickly and hop into bed with him for the best night's sleep in a long time. We all wake up early with the sun shining brightly in our hotel room. We are all so excited about our big day at Magic Kingdom — who wouldn't want to wake up early? The only thing that could have made it better would be having Andrew here, but I know we will get our time. For the moment this is amazing and I won't let anything spoil it. I call home to check in with Lauren.

"Andrew had a great night, don't worry, Mom. I told you I will call you if anything happens. I love him too."

"I know. Thank you! You will never know what this means to me, to our family." I stop and thank God, not only because I was able to make it, but for Lauren, because without her I could never have come. I don't know who is more excited at this point: me, Justin or Matthew!

It is a gorgeous day: sunny, cloudless sky and perfect spring temperature. Walking into Disney World is always impressive, but we could be walking into a local carnival for all I care. I am just thrilled to have this time together, this opportunity for some genuine fun. We take off as if we were being chased to start hitting rides. Before long, it's time for lunch and we grab the usual amusement park fried fare as we listen to Matthew talk excitedly about what rides he wants to do next. My cell phone rings and my heart sinks. My first thought is that it's Lauren and something has happened with Andrew.

"Hello, Mrs. Akin? Yes, this is Dr. Morgan. I have some bad news: something has started to grow in Andrew's white line. It's a different bug than what was growing in his red line. This infection is a gram-positive bug (a bug from outside his body). He is going to need more serious antibiotics and will also need to be admitted immediately. There is some concern because this particular bug has the potential to cause damage to his liver and brain, so he needs to have a CAT scan to make sure everything looks OK. In addition, we are scheduling him for surgery to remove his central line from his chest. Since he has a double-line infection, we feel it is best to pull the line, keep him on the antibiotics until both infections are cleared and then put a new central line in. What time can you be down here to get checked in? . . . Mrs. Akin, are you there?"

"Yes, I'm sorry, I'm here. Um, well, I won't be able to check him in because I am in Florida but our nurse, Lauren, can bring him down right away and I will catch the next flight home."

Trying to get an airplane ticket out of Florida on the Saturday before Easter is almost impossible. All I could get was a first-class ticket on Delta with a connection in Atlanta. Justin calmly says, "It's OK. You know Lauren is taking great care of him. She'll get him down there and checked in; she works there for God's sake."

"I know," I sob, "but I feel terrible. I should have never come."

"There was no way to know. The doctors told you everything was negative. It's OK, just take a deep breath. Everything is going to be all right. Call me when you get to the hospital." I kneel down to talk to Matthew.

"I love you, Matthew Man. I am so sorry I have to leave so quickly, but Baby Andrew is sick and needs Mommy to come home. But I know you will have a blast with Daddy."

Within two hours of receiving the call from the doctor outside of Space Mountain, I am on a plane heading home. *Damn it, I cannot believe this is happening again. This roller coaster just won't stop.* I look out the window as we fly among the clouds and I feel a tad closer to God, I'm not sure why. I find myself begging and pleading for help, for patience, for strength. *God, please spare my sweet Baby Andrew, please keep him safe. We are trying so hard. I just don't know what to do anymore.*

I check in with Lauren by phone as soon as I land. I know Andrew is in the best hands possible but not being there is torture. Driving to Children's I replay the last forty-eight hours. Fact is stranger than fiction. I am completely out of breath by the time I reach Nine West; our second home. I open the door to see one of my favorite things: a huge Andrew Bear smile. He doesn't look sick at all. He begins to bounce up and down when he sees me, something he does when he is happy, and that makes me happy. For all the days and nights I have spent in this hospital, dying to get out, at that moment I could not have been any happier than to be standing right there. I immediately jump in the shower to scrub off all the dirt and germs from the outside world. As disappointed as I was to leave Matthew and Justin, I am as thankful to see how well Andrew is doing right now. Dressed in my pajamas and finally all clean, I hug Andrew and then Lauren, and remind myself never to leave again.

I have our bed made up in no time and Andrew and I tuck in together like so many nights before. I am surprised how long we sleep in, but then again it is Easter Sunday, and holidays are very quiet in the hospital as they try and send as many patients home as possible, even if it's just for the night.

I think we would still be sleeping, but we are woken up by six doctors standing over us — apparently the attending doctor and a bunch of residents. I listen closely as I rub my eyes.

"We are pleased with how well Andrew is responding to the new antibiotics, so at this point, we are going to hold off on the CAT scan. But we have moved his surgery up: it will be today around noon, OK, Mrs. Akin? We want to get those lines out of his body to make sure he can clear both infections completely."

"OK, I understand, thank you." They all turn and walk out as quickly as they came. I lie back down on our bench/bed next to my sleeping son. "Well Andrew, the bad news is you won't be going outside to hunt for Easter eggs today, partly because it's snowing and also because you're sick, but the good news is after they take your central line out today, it will be out for a few weeks, so you will finally be able to take a normal bath! I know you don't understand what I am saying, but you do understand this." I give him a huge hug and kiss.

Chapter 10

What lies behind us and what lies before us are tiny matters
compared to what lies within us.
—Ralph Waldo Emerson

May 2008

*J*ustin and Matthew returned from Disney and Andrew and I finally got discharged. We were all together again under one roof and it felt so good. But before long, somehow despite our best attempts to stay healthy and keep things as clean as possible, Matthew and I both woke up sick. The roller coaster just keeps going. Every time it seems like things start to go our way, inevitably something like this happens. To say this makes life hard would be an understatement; it is literally a life and death situation for Andrew.

So today, when Matthew first wakes up and runs into our room with a cough and a runny nose, Justin and I immediately fly out of bed and go into crisis mode. Justin grabs Matthew and puts him in the car and heads straight over to my parents immediately. Meanwhile, I put on gloves and a mask and start wiping every door handle, light switch and toy I can get my hands on while Andrew is still sleeping. I strip the sheets off our bed and Matthew's bed. Once Justin returns from dropping Matthew off, he will be on full-time Andrew duty, and I will be exiled to the basement. I hate that we have to rush Matthew out of the house, and that I too have to go in hiding; our entire lives get turned upside down for a simple cold.

"Honey are you doing OK down there? Can I bring you anything?" Justin hollers down.

"No, but thanks. I'm going to try and sleep. Does Andrew seem OK? Do you think he caught anything?"

"So far, so good. Get some sleep and I will check on you later." And the basement door shuts with a boom. Thank goodness Andrew seems OK! This is ridiculous; what else can we be doing to protect him? We have gone above and beyond what the doctors suggest. We even pulled Matthew out of nursery school after Christmas despite the fact that he loved it, and we loved it. We were too afraid of the germs he could bring home to his brother. But Matthew still seems to be sick fairly often. Now I am, too, and I'm Andrew's primary caregiver. "Please," I cry out loud, "please God, help me. I just don't know what to do anymore." My tears continue until I finally fall asleep in our dark, cool basement.

The bugs finally clear. Matthew comes home from my parents' house and I emerge from the basement. Andrew looks great; thankfully he never caught what we had. Matthew is completely back to his old self. Within just minutes of being around my boys again, my heart feels whole, and I am recharged: good to go for at least another hundred miles. Which is good because it's time to check back into Children's. Andrew will be having his new double line placed in preparation for his second bone marrow transplant.

It has been a dream come true having no line for the past few weeks. For the whole time since Andrew was first diagnosed at ten weeks old, he has had a central line. It has been good to have access for lab draws and medicines without using needles, but it comes with a drawbacks as well. Andrew has had to take modified baths to keep the line and dressing completely dry. Plus, even just sitting in his diaper poses a risk because he can pull the line out of his chest. Weekly sterile dressing changes, cap changes, flushing the line, hooking it up to numerous medicines daily — not having to deal with all that has been a treat for me as well. However, my favorite thing about Andrew not having his central line was having Matthew and Andrew be able to take a bath together. The bathtub full of bubbles and toys and both boys in there playing, splashing and having fun together: I could sit on the edge of the tub and watch them forever. They both splash me and Matthew makes bubble mustaches on himself and his brother. It is heavenly to see them interact; truly a gift. But now that fun is over and that normality is gone.

Finally, the news we have been so desperately waiting for: we have a donor. A twenty-four-year-old woman is the best match for our son, and she is willing to donate.

Even though we understand how the process works, we are completely in awe. Soon after Andrew was diagnosed, we held our first bone marrow drive, and we were humbled by the hundreds of perfect strangers who signed up because they heard Andrew's story. Conversely, we were shocked that some people were no longer interested in joining once they heard they were probably not going to be a match for Andrew. I wish I could call this young woman up right now and say thank you: *thank you for being on the registry, thank you for giving our son a second chance at life, thank you for being so selfless.* How do you begin to say thank you for providing life? You never know when you or someone you love might be in the same shoes we're in, waiting for the kindness of a complete stranger. I hope I will get the call some day to potentially save someone's life.

Just like that, our time at home is over and Andrew and I are in the hospital again, for his new central line. Even though this was a scheduled admission, I still dreaded it. There could never be enough time at home all together. I call Justin to check in.

"Hi, how's Matthew doing? Everything going OK?"

"Yes, honey, we are fine. What's going on there?"

"Well, good news first: we have a private room and Kelly is our nurse tonight. Surgery and anesthesia just came by for the standard meet and sign your life away. Andrew is scheduled for first thing in the morning, thankfully. What did you guys do today?"

"Matthew and I played outside until dark. He had lots of fun riding his bike up and down the street as fast as his little legs could pedal with his favorite rain boots on." I can't help but laugh as I picture my adventurous son zooming down the street with the training wheels bobbing on either side.

"Please make sure and give him a big hug and kiss for me."

"I will, I always do."

"I know, just an extra one."

"How's Andrew doing?"

"Great! The nurse got his IV in on the first stick, so between that, our private room and the fact that we are first for surgery tomorrow, I am starting to feel VIP."

Justin laughs. "Yeah I'm sure. I love you."

"I love you too, and will call in the morning once he is out of surgery." Andrew and I snuggle in our hospital bed together, like so many nights before. I say my prayers, which have become quite simple these days. *God, you know what I want: a healthy, long-term survivor, so perhaps the best thing to pray for is what I need to make that happen.* I give thanks for my long list of blessings and fall asleep before I finish.

I have no idea how long we have been asleep as I try to sit up without waking Andrew. I look to see what time it is and immediately make eye contact with our nurse, who gives me a look I have seen before that says, "I'm sorry, but we have no other beds." I glance at the cheap plastic clock on the wall and see it is 4:00 a.m. Just then the patient gets wheeled into the room, and she is screaming. She has sickle-cell disease and is in what they call a "pain crisis." Each scream is louder than the next. She moans and hollers and soon wakes up Andrew. I am so annoyed I could scream bloody murder. *What is wrong with this picture? My son has no immune system, and now we are sharing a room with a girl and her family who don't need to be concerned about germs. Not to mention the fact that she is screaming in pain, and I am trying to keep my eleven-month-old baby sleeping as long as possible since he can't have anything to eat or drink until after his surgery. Now he is up and hungry, and I can't feed him.*

"I'm sorry," our nurse whispers in my ear.

"It's OK," I say. "I know it's not your fault." What really makes me mad is that there are empty rooms on the other side of the floor waiting to be redone when we could use the space now. They told me the whole floor was getting redone but it is almost a year later and nothing has happened. Those rooms sit empty. To top it all off, the girl's family just left her, and now she is all alone, screaming even louder. I wouldn't believe this stuff if I didn't see it with my own eyes.

Familiar but never fun is the surgery waiting room. I pace the room, drink my coffee, check my watch and start over again. Finally, I hear our last name and head to the receptionist desk as fast as my feet will carry me.

"Andrew is out of surgery and doing well. You can see him, but first the surgeon would like to talk with you. Please step into this room."

"Well, we tried to go back in on the left side where Andrew's previous central line was but we ran into trouble, so we ended up going in on the right side this time. I just wanted to let you know since we always try to use the previous entrance and exit sites to cut down on scars."

"OK, is there going to be an issue or problem?"

"No, it should be fine. He will just have those extra bandages where we tried to go in." What can I really say at this point; it's already done. Of course I am not happy about it, but I just want to see Andrew right now more than anything else.

"Can you please just take me to see him?" The surgeon nods and I follow him to the door.

"Andrew Bear, it's mommy. I'm here, Buddy, I love you." It always takes me a minute to look at the wounds that have been made on my baby's body. I assess the stitches, the blood, the lines and the bruises and take a deep breath. Now is not the time for me to cry; I'll do that later, in private. Now, I scoop my baby up off the gurney, wrap him back up in his blanket and begin to feed him his milk. "Thank you, God for safely bringing me my baby back," I whisper. "I love him and need him."

"I'm telling you: something is wrong," I insist. "Andrew had no breathing issues before we came in for this admission. He has been doing great and his oxygen saturation leading up to surgery has been perfect — a non-issue. They must have done something during surgery."

"No, I really don't think that is possible."

"Well, I don't care what you think," I calmly say to our resident, "I am telling you they did." We proceed to stare each other down for another minute or two before he just turns and walks out. I call Justin.

"Andrew is on blow-by oxygen and that seems to be enough, but I am telling you they screwed something up when they were in there today!"

"OK, just calm down, I will be there shortly." I start talking to myself and anyone who comes into our room or will listen. I feel so frustrated because I don't know what it could be but I do know something is wrong. It is not a coincidence that he's having breathing problems after they tried to surgically insert a plastic tube into his chest.

"For what it's worth, I agree," our nurse pipes in.

The next twenty-four hours go from bad to worse. Andrew continues to struggle with his oxygen saturation and the blow by oxygen is no longer enough to support him. Try taping a nasal cannula in your baby's nose — we couldn't get one side taped before he had the other side ripped off his face.

"Andrew, I know you don't like this, Buddy, but you need it. Please let Mommy help you." After a dose of Benadryl to help him sleep and with me rocking him, he finally falls asleep and I can stop holding his hands down.

"We have scheduled a fluoroscopy today," our doctor says. "That should help us get a better idea of what is going on."

"OK, but I know it has to be something from his surgery," I insist.

"Dr. David is one of the best surgeons in this hospital. He has literally put in hundreds of central lines, and we have never seen this before."

So, is that the explanation we are going with? I thought to myself. *Sorry, we don't know what caused it, but it couldn't have been us since we never have before.* We head down to the X-ray department, and as with every test Andrew has had done, I am right there with him. This time I have to do more than just hold him in place; I have to make him cry so they can see his lungs and diaphragm fully expand and contract. I pinch my son's arm, trying to get him to start screaming. On the screen I see that his left diaphragm barely moves. I'm not sure if my tears are for the fact that I had to pinch my baby until he cried, or the fact that I can clearly see his left diaphragm is not working at all.

After getting back to our room, it takes us both a while to calm down. Andrew and I are both in tears but clearly for different reasons. I am furious and I don't want to hear another person tell me this didn't happen from his central line placement, because it did. *It might not be something you see very often but now you are, so take a good look because you did this to my son.*

Andrew remains on oxygen support throughout the weekend. By Monday morning we are able to decrease the oxygen a little and that is giving me great hope. I am pleased to see one of my favorite doctors stop by. He is calm and friendly and generally seems to see the glass half full, which I can surely use right now.

"Mom, I wanted you to know that I did a bunch of research over the past weekend and found a handful of documented cases of partial paralysis of the diaphragm being caused by central line surgery. In the cases documented it got better on its own, and I am hopeful Andrew will continue to improve as well."

"Thank you, thank you so much, Dr. Woods. I can't tell you how much I appreciate your spending the time to research this." I knew it had to be related. I know it was an accident and that with every procedure, every test, every medicine, there is a risk. But quite frankly I am tired of all the risks. I just don't want anyone else to touch my sweet baby.

This disease sucks.

Chapter 11

Without faith, nothing is possible. With it, nothing is impossible.
—Mary McLeod Bethune

June 2008

$\mathcal{E}$xcited isn't the word. I think anxious is probably more like it. Oh I don't know, I think we are both excited. We should be: Andrew is about to have his second bone marrow transplant. It is hard to fathom that this is his second one in less than a year — he hasn't even turned one yet. But Justin and I are very hopeful. This transplant is going to be different, because this time Andrew will be receiving bone marrow instead of cord cells.

"Remind me again why they used cord cells the first time," my best friend Mel says.

"Well, the doctors wanted to use bone marrow for Andrew's first transplant as well, but there was no match on the registry at the time. Ideally, we would have waited a while longer to see if something popped up, but since Andrew's HLH started to flare up again, he needed to have his transplant immediately. Cord cells sit in a freezer, which makes them far more accessible than bone marrow. It goes without saying that Justin and I were devastated when Andrew's first transplant failed, but I have come to terms with it. The cord cells bought us time, and if that was their only purpose then it worked. Now we have a great match."

"Do you think it's going to work this time?"

"Yes. I know it is going to work; the odds are stacked in our favor," I say confidently. The previous experience taught me so much. Now I know what we are facing, and that makes me feel much better. No matter how much you read you can't begin to prepare yourself for that type of experience, you just have to live it.

I talk to my mother on the phone.

"Yes, Mom, he has to go through all the same bodily function tests as before. They use them as an indicator of his health before the transplant, so if he sustains any permanent organ damage, we will have a starting point to compare with."

"But it seems silly, since it has only been a few months since he had them all."

"I agree, Mom, but those are the rules."

"What about the insurance? Have you heard yet if his second transplant is approved?"

"No, not yet, but our bone marrow coordinator told me not to worry about it. They won't postpone his transplant, regardless of insurance approval. Don't worry, Mom, it's going to work. He is going to get better and we are going to get through this."

"What are you going to do about his birthday?" my mom asks hesitantly. "I am sure you two will still be in the bone marrow unit."

"The same thing I have been doing all along: be flexible. I will bring the party here, just like his baptism. It will be different, but wonderful nonetheless. I will not let this disease or this place stop me from celebrating." Just because Andrew's sick doesn't mean he doesn't deserve what his brother had, or better yet, what we had planned for him before this horrible disease struck our family.

Moving back into the bone marrow unit feels eerily familiar; we are even in the same room as before. Is that a good sign or a bad sign? In my cheesy, crafty mom fashion I come up with new decorations to make it special, to make it ours: to make it home. I begin hanging my white twinkle lights around the perimeter of the room, and before I can get the words out, Justin has a piece of tape ready for me.

I am especially pleased with the new family posters I made. I knew Justin thought I was crazy to make new ones, but I wanted to. I like these posters and I believe they're very important. They will make an impact on every person who enters our room, and that is what I want. The posters are clearly made out of love, and while they would never win an art show, that's not the point. I want people to realize that Andrew is more than a hospital number or another sick child to see in rounds. Andrew is a brother, a son and a grandson. He is loved and cherished and needed! I want everyone to stop and look, and feel the love that our family shares; to realize that his life is important. I continue unpacking until I am stopped by Justin's laughter.

"What is that?" he asks.

"Oh, that's my shower caddy."

"Why do you have a shower caddy?" he asks, laughing the whole time.

"Hey, you might think it's funny, but I've learned a few things since my last stay here. Try carrying all your bathroom supplies, plus your towel and clean clothes to the parent lounge: it's tough. I would always drop something, so this way I have it all together. Remember, not everyone gets to shower in the privacy of their own bathroom," I joke. Sharing a bathroom with strangers is gross; it is the one thing that I have not gotten used to — and I don't think I will.

When we are finished organizing and unpacking our stuff, Justin and I sit down on the bed and hold Andrew between us. We can't stop telling him how proud we are of him, and he just laughs.

"Tell Lindsay thanks again for letting Matthew stay and play with his friends outside." I know it was more fun than coming down here, even though I miss not having that extra time with him. Justin slides open the first of the two doors that separate us from the outside world. I am still sitting on our bed, holding Andrew as Justin slides open the second door and quietly walks out.

"Andrew, you and your brother Matthew are the luckiest boys in the whole world. You have the best daddy ever!"

Coming into this transplant with one already behind us is a double-edged sword. We both feel so much more prepared, but that extra experience and knowledge does not come for free. I have seen way too many horrific things over the last nine months. I have learned about procedures, drugs, machines and diseases I never knew existed. I have heard codes called, seen parents leave their children for days and watched in horror as someone was rushed to the PICU. And of course, there's death. You don't forget the sight of parents walking out of their child's room for the very last time, seeing the nurses clear the hallway so the body can be taken to the morgue, hearing the sobs and feeling the grief among all of us who live on the floor. The worst part is knowing we can't imagine their pain but thanking God it is not our child.

But Justin and I feel encouraged, too. Along with all the bad stuff, we have learned so much about Andrew's disease, about the bone marrow transplant process, and about complications, risks and side effects, and that makes us feel more able to help our son. Andrew has shown us he is here to stay. He has already overcome so many obstacles I know he will get through this as well. His name means "brave and courageous" and that is exactly what he is.

Words cannot begin to describe the pain and grief of being away from Matthew this year. I don't think I will ever get over it, because that time is gone and I can never get it back. But today I get to see him! Not for long, but I am thrilled to have as much time as possible. Matthew barely makes it through the door and I almost tackle him to the ground with hugs and kisses. Within minutes he realizes that the curtain that hangs in his brother's room for privacy can be used as a great stage. And before our eyes, Matthew the entertainer whisks the curtain back, steps forward and we are greeted with the cutest singing and dancing little boy I have ever seen. You can feel the joy and laughter fill the room; it is wonderful. Upon finishing his routine, we all break into applause at the same time and Matthew bows and says thank you with a huge grin on his face. Now off to lunch. Justin stayed behind in the hospital with Andrew so Matthew and I could go out for lunch. We walk to a nearby café just down from the hospital. It is a beautiful day and the sun on my face feels powerful and healing, but nothing feels better than holding Matthew's warm little hand. I wish I could stop time — just freeze this moment with the two of us together. I have not seen Matthew very much lately because he has been spending a week at a time between my parents and Justin's mom's house in Dallas as we prepare for Andrew's second transplant. We did this to try to provide a better routine and schedule for him until we can all be back home together again. While we are both so grateful to have the help, it breaks our hearts to be away from him.

On our way back from lunch we pass two fountains, which he loves! He wants to throw a penny into both so I dig into my wallet for some change. It doesn't take long for the first penny to go in, and he says, "God, please bring my mommy home." Before I can wipe away my tears, the second penny is in, and Matthew asks God, again so matter-of-factly, to please help Baby Andrew get better. I could not be more proud of this little boy. He continues to amaze me, and the fact that I am losing so much valuable time with him in an effort to try and save my other son is so unfair to him. I don't want to hear another person say another stupid, rhetorical statement like *God doesn't give you more than you can handle* or *hang in there*. Right now I am exhausted and scared. I just want Andrew to get better once and for all, and I want to be home caring for and loving my sweet Matthew Man, as I should be.

And then we wait patiently while somewhere in this vast country of ours, a perfect stranger goes into the hospital to have a needle stuck into her hip bone to harvest her bone marrow. Then another perfect stranger will take this life-saving marrow and fly it to St. Louis for Andrew. If this does not make you believe in the kindness of strangers, then I don't know what will. The plane carrying Andrew's marrow is scheduled to land in St. Louis around 6 p.m., which means we should be able to start the transplant around 11 p.m. Before Andrew can receive the marrow, it has to go to the lab to have several tests run on it. The doctors requested at least 2.5 million cells, but we received 8.9 million cells! Thank you angel donor — because of this, they have decided to give Andrew a little more than half of the marrow and save the rest in case we need a boost later down the road. We were thrilled to hear there was so much. This is the best gift Andrew will ever receive!

Andrew has received his pre-transplant medications, is hooked up to the various monitors and now we just wait patiently for the marrow to arrive. Finally, the double doors to the bone marrow unit open and in walks the lab tech with a ziplock bag with Andrew's marrow in it. I grab my camera, just like the first time, and begin snapping pictures. Even though we have done this before it is not any less amazing. I check the clock: 11:36 p.m. Justin and I watch closely as new life begins to drip into Andrew's body from a pint-sized hospital-grade bag filled with what looks like blood. If you didn't know better, you would think he was just getting a blood transfusion but only we know that it is more precious than blood.

Andrew just lies on his bed, sucking on his pacifier and snuggling his lovie during the infusion of his new marrow. As he laughs and sits up, trying to pull at the twenty or so lines coming out of his body, it seems impossible that his life is in danger. Today marks a chapter — a new beginning, and these new cells are going to provide the healthy immune system Andrew so desperately needs.

Chapter 12

If at first you don't succeed, try, try again.

—Unknown

June 5, 2008

*T*oday is Andrew's first birthday. One year ago today I delivered Andrew via C-section. He weighed seven pounds and nine ounces, just like his brother. He had been scheduled to be delivered on June sixth but he decided he wanted to come on June fifth instead. I could not have been happier, and despite this horrific disease, I would not trade him for anything. I surely did not foresee spending his first birthday in the bone marrow unit as I didn't even know what a bone marrow unit was, but I have no doubt this will be the most special birthday we ever celebrate. Through Andrew's illness I have learned so much about life, death, faith, patience, and most importantly: what really matters. Life is for living — today, not tomorrow or next week — but today.

Andrew doesn't know he is sick, he doesn't know he has a life-threatening disease, or what chemo is. He doesn't realize he has already had two bone marrow transplants in less than a year. What he does know is that he is loved. He knows he is treasured and needed. It's not a coincidence that Andrew is by far the happiest baby I have ever known. And while today will be filled with balloons, presents, cake, food, friends and family, it is really the love that Andrew gives to us and that we give to him that we are celebrating. Even though no one but Justin and I will get to touch Andrew or hold him today, I know without a doubt that as our family stands behind the thick glass doors that separate us they will be happier than they ever thought possible.

Andrew is dressed in the most adorable light blue shortall with a cupcake appliquéd on the front. The white Peter Pan collar lies perfectly around his neck and he looks beautiful. His checks are chubby from the continual steroids but that helps make him look extra healthy. The large gym mat we normally use for therapy has been converted to our stage, covered in a clean sheet. Andrew sits front and center, buckled into his little booster seat. Justin and I are sitting next to him on the mat, and two prouder parents there could not be. I set the A-shaped homemade cake on Andrew's tray; we give him a minute and then show him he can touch and eat it. Andrew digs in with joy and laughter, making a mess, as every one-year-old should. We all laughed together. Today we celebrated our son's first birthday in the bone marrow unit and it could not have been a better day. Today I finally cried tears of joy, tears of thanksgiving. Andrew has come so far, he has taught us so many life lessons, he has already changed the world I live in for the better, and for that I am honored to be his mom.

Things continue to go well and Andrew seems unfazed by his second bone marrow transplant in less than a year. We patiently wait for his new cells to move in and start working. Until they do, he remains on fluid restriction, which was a big deal during the first transplant since I had no warning. However, thanks to my ingenious idea of putting baby food in a bottle for him to drink, fluid restriction is no longer a headache.

Our days are similar and repetitive. I often joke and say, "Look, Andrew: it's Big Ben . . . and Parliament!" which is from Chevy Chase's movie *European Vacation*, when they get stuck driving around the round-about and can't get over. I know he doesn't understand a word I am saying but it makes me laugh every time, silly mommy. Andrew's hair has started to fall out again, and despite the fact that this is the second time in his short life it has happened, I am not any more used to it. Waking up to a pile of my son's hair on our pillow is heartbreaking, and knowing it was going to happen doesn't make it any easier.

We keep busy each day with visits from our friends: the occupational therapist, physical therapist, music therapist and child life therapist. It is always a bright spot in our day when Andrew gets to play with one of them because it is someone different to interact with besides me. Andrew is very social and loves people, so this gives him a chance to share his joyful and happy personality with others. Everyone comments that Andrew is the happiest baby they have ever met, and that just melts my heart. Justin and I have talked about it. Did God make Andrew that way because He knew his life was going to be short? That is a very painful thought, but one that can't be avoided.

From the very beginning of Andrew's illness I have kept track of everything. That three-ring binder has become part of my daily ritual, as much as brushing my teeth and getting dressed. I start every morning by going over his labs from the previous night and record them. I know our nurses must track everything as well, even his oral and IV meds must be accounted for, but my book is more than just a record of labs. Tracking Andrew's urine and stool output is also something that I do and record. Without even noticing I was doing it, I began to guess how much his diaper would weigh before I set it on the scale. I am getting quite good at it and have turned it into a game with one of our nurses. She knows as soon as I change Andrew's diaper it is time to guess. Today is no different: she takes the diaper, holds it in her hand, and says, "Twenty-seven." I weigh it in my hand.

"No . . . thirty-three." We stand side by side in the bathroom watching the dial on the scale as I set Andrew's diaper down — thirty-two.

"Gosh, you're getting good at this," she laughs.

"What can I say? Practice makes perfect!" I grab my pen and write it down on today's "Ins and Outs" sheet. I keep track of everything, down to how much every diaper weighs, not just because the nurses need the information but because I can. It is my job to be Andrew's advocate, to be on top of his care in any and every way I can. It is the least I can do for my son as he battles for his life.

After twenty-four days of being in Room 2 in the bone marrow unit, we are finally going home. Andrew is starting to engraft and is doing great. Of course I am thrilled to be going home, but there is always a slight sense of fear at leaving. Living in the hospital provides an unspoken comfort because you know your nurse is right outside the room and you are only a button press away from help.

Going home means now I am the primary nurse; I am mixing medicine, changing lines and evaluating every little thing. To say this is a big responsibility would not begin to cover it. But being at home brings so many comforts, so many joys and little things that most people take for granted. Realistically, I know our nurses and doctors are only a phone call away. There's also our home health nurse. She was assigned to us right after Andrew first got diagnosed and we hit it off immediately — she is awesome. She comes to the house to do labs in between hospital visits, she delivers medicine and teaches us how to use all of Andrew's home medical equipment. Our nurses do so much more than just administer medicine; they offer encouragement, help and often their shoulder to cry on. They are often as helpful to us parents as they are to our children.

I cannot begin to explain how wonderful it is to be home. I soak up everything I have missed: stepping onto the floor and not having to have shoes on, being able to walk into our kitchen and grab a snack, having privacy. But more than that, being home means Andrew is well enough to leave the hospital. It means he is starting to engraft and his new cells are moving in. It means he is on his way to finally beating HLH once and for all.

Even though we have walked this path before, the days and weeks after the transplant are not any easier. We hope and pray every day that the new cells from his donor are working, that they are happy to be in his body and his body is happy to have them. One of our biggest fears is graft-versus-host disease (GVHD), which is one of the most common complications of bone marrow transplants, especially with bone marrow versus cord cells. While we wait, we stay busy with clinic visits several times a week, Andrew's home care, and of course playing with our sweet and adventurous Matthew. We try to find normality in a most abnormal situation.

Lying in bed this morning I tune in to all the sounds and feelings of our family. I stretch out in our big king-sized bed and feel Gilligan lying at my feet. I listen to the sounds Andrew makes from his crib to tell us he is awake. I hear Matthew downstairs, which tells me I should probably go investigate. As soon as I reach the bottom stair I notice a kitchen chair sitting next to the fridge. *Hmmm.* I slowly walk towards the living/play room and what do I spy? My sweet Matthew Man sitting on the floor surrounded by a dozen eggs, a plastic measuring cup, box of Bisquick and a large bowl.

"What are you doing, Matthew?"

"I'm making paypays, Mommy." Paypays is his way of saying pancakes. I can't help but laugh.

"Oh, thank you. It looks like you have almost everything already done." I quickly call for Justin to come see. With Andrew in tow we come and admire what our smart, independent son had done. Matthew and I love to cook together and making pancakes is a regular occurrence whenever I am home. Of course I have to get a picture of this and I grab my camera. Andrew sits next to his brother, bouncing up and down with delight, as usual.

It is hard for me to fathom all that has happened in the last year. On that sunny August afternoon when I went in to get Andrew up from his nap and he was yellow, I never saw this coming. I guess most critical illnesses don't give much warning, but this one surely came out of left field.

I have argued, begged and pleaded with God but to no avail; He did not magically heal Andrew. Listening to people talk about their faith and deliver platitudes like *God has not abandoned you* and *He must have chosen you because you're so strong* has made me want to scream. Please. You don't get it. God does not have a hotline, because if He did I would have called it a hundred times by now. He does not work for us because we pray more or harder. God has a plan, and it doesn't always make sense. Often it doesn't make any sense, but accepting it anyway is what faith really is. I finally get it. Faith means not giving up on God because we feel things are not fair, or they're not going our way. We must remain faithful that there is a bigger plan. I don't know what His plan is right now, but I am remaining faithful that it will reveal itself soon.

Chapter 13

If you are going through hell, keep going.
—Winston Churchill

August 2008

"It's not his engraftment we're worried about now, it's GVHD."

"OK, we are not trying to be difficult but can you go over this again? It is still pretty new for your dad and me. We thought everything was good. His engraftment had been stable around 85%, which is what we were praying for, right?"

"Yes, Mom, you're right. Unlike his last transplant, his new cells have engrafted and Andrew's bone marrow remains mostly donor cells, which is what he needs to beat HLH. However, we remain cautious of graft-versus-host disease, which is one of the biggest complications post-transplant. The easiest way I know to explain it is this: when the new cells — the cells from the donor — come into Andrew's body, they can identify his cells as being different. Once the cells realize they are in a foreign place they might launch an attack on Andrew's tissue and organs. And because he has been immune-suppressed for so long from the chemo, his body can't launch a counterattack. This is called graft-versus-host disease (GVHD). The 'graft' is the donated bone marrow and the 'host' is the bone marrow recipient. Does that make sense?" I ask, looking at my parents' puzzled faces.

"Yes," they say in unison. "So . . . does he have that?"

"Well, I'm not sure, but to be honest my gut says yes. He has had a rash off and on lately, but it has been in different spots on his body. Our doctor doesn't seem too concerned, because Andrew has not had it on the palms of his hands or the bottom of his feet, which would be textbook GVHD. The problem is that they classify GVHD into two categories: acute being within the first hundred days after the transplant and chronic being everything after a hundred days. And while that is helpful, it is really just a guide."

"What do you mean, Kristin?" my mom asks, concerned.

"I mean that HLH is rare and bone marrow transplants are very new in the world of medicine. No one really knows for sure what Andrew's body is going to do with these new cells from his donor; only time will tell."

"You sound pessimistic," my dad says.

"I'm not; just realistic. The more I learn about bone marrow transplants the more I realize there is so much we still don't know. The fact is, while this was our only option to save Andrew's life, it doesn't come for free or without major risks and complications. We take away his immune system because it is broken and will kill him otherwise, but in the process the drugs we are giving him to try and save him and the new cells he has received can be just as much of a risk, if not more," I say, holding back my tears. My mom and dad each reach out to hug me. There is nothing to say.

We have been in the outpatient clinic for hours today, and my frustration mounts as the time passes.

"Look, it's day +75 and Andrew's rash is getting worse," I insist.

"I know you don't think it's GVHD, but I do, and I'm really worried. The topical steroid cream is not working, and Andrew is clearly feeling much worse. He is itching all the time and his skin is beet red. We have to do something about this — today." I can tell our doctor wants to get me off his back.

"OK, I will call down to the dermatology department and have you seen by one of the senior doctors."

"Thank you," I say firmly. "I'm just not comfortable sitting on this anymore. We have given it more than enough time to get better, whether it was a random virus or whatever else it could be. It's getting worse and I need answers." He hands me the script and off we go. It used to be hard for me to speak up. In the beginning, I was intimidated — but not anymore. After all this time in the hospital I have come to realize that doctors, no matter how experienced, put their pants on one leg at a time, just like me. Besides, I have always known that no matter what, no one will love and look out for my son as well as Justin and I will.

When we step into the dermatology clinic, my heart sinks. At first glance it might look nice: spacious and colorful, full of big windows and cartoons playing in the background. But as the mother of a bone marrow patient, all I see is the people and the potential germs that put my son at risk. The receptionist is less than friendly and won't accommodate us at all even when I explain our situation. I tell her Andrew has no immune system and must be kept in isolation because he just had his second bone marrow transplant two months ago, but she has no interest in what I am saying. I firmly let her know we will be waiting outside the clinic, in the hallway, which I feel is the safest place considering they won't put us in a room for isolation.

"Well, if we call your name and you don't hear us then you will miss the appointment," she says.

"OK, look: I am not a walk-in," I calmly say. "If you look at the script I just gave you, you will see that it was written by our doctor today, and he wants us seen today."

She and I look at each other, and she simply says, "I will call your name when we're ready." Standing in the hall, listening for our name, I can't decide if I want to scream or cry. Matthew has been so patient today, but he is clearly ready to go home, play or do something other than sit in a hospital, and I don't blame him because so am I. I let him go into the corner of the waiting room where I can see him and play some type of video game they have built into the wall. In the meantime, poor Andrew is sopping wet and I lay him back in his stroller to use as a makeshift changing table. In between changing Andrew's wet diaper and clothes and watching Matthew playing in the waiting room, I look down at my watch and see that an hour has gone by. I am about to walk out, because enough is enough, when I hear, "Andrew Akin?"

"Yes, we're coming," I yell. "Matthew, come on, Buddy, it's our turn." I reach my hand out to him, making sure Andrew's blanket stays over the top of his stroller, doing my best to keep him isolated from people as much as possible. "Open your hands, Matthew." He knows what to do with the hand sanitizer without me saying another word.

"Hi, I'm Doctor Smith, and I am one of the residents in the dermatology department right now. If you don't mind, can you please give me Andrew's history? It says here you are worried about a rash . . ." I sit back in the stiff plastic chair in our small examination room that looks like so many others we have been in. I can't help but chuckle to myself. This resident is so serious and thinks I am just another mom who's overly concerned about some baby rash. *I am about to blow the doors off this doctor.*

"Well, where do you want me to start? Are you familiar with his disease, hemophagocytic lymphohistiocytosis, and graft-versus-host disease, and do you understand the severity of his compromised immune system?" He stares at me as he realizes that I am not your run-of-the-mill mom and this is not your run-of-the-mill baby. In fact, he looks like he just hit the jackpot. This is his lucky day; he is going to learn a hell of a lot. So I start with my basic speech about HLH and Andrew's first failed bone marrow transplant and his second transplant. I pull out my binder and open it to his list of medications and the spreadsheet we have created to keep track of what medicines he gets when. The discussion continues until I think he is either worn out from me talking or realizes it is going to take him a while to download all of this information so he'd better go. He gets up and excuses himself, and I am left with my boys.

"Matthew, I love you and am so proud of you. You have done such a great job today. I promise we will be done soon and I will take you to the train store tomorrow to pick out some new trains. How does that sound?" I know the answer before he gives it, but I love hearing his sweet voice anyway: "Good, Mommy."

Within minutes of meeting the dermatologist, I was ready to storm out, but since I waited so long, I stayed a little longer even though short of healing Andrew on the spot, there wasn't much this doctor could say that I wanted to hear. Thankfully, the conversation was brief and we were on our way out of there and home.

After buckling my boys into their car seats, I drive around and around the parking garage until we come to the pay station. My brain will not stop replaying what just happened; I am about to burst with anger. I cannot believe she had the nerve to reprimand my son — and for what?

He was sitting in the chair next to me, not talking, looking through one of his books when she just up and says, "Now listen to me, little boy. You need to keep your mouth shut while your mommy and I are talking. Do you understand?" Talk about being caught off guard! I didn't even have a response, which is so unlike me. And then she thinks Andrew's rash is just contact dermatitis. What, are you kidding me?

As she goes through the list of questions about soap, detergent and lotion, I am trying to tell her: "It's not dermatitis. He just had a second bone marrow transplant. I think it's graft-versus-host disease." But she was not having any of it. *Really? You don't think you should entertain the thought since he has had two bone marrow transplants in less than a year?* Damn, if I never see her again, it will be too soon.

"Look, Mommy, coal cars!"

"Yes, you're right, Buddy. Thank you for pointing those out to me," I say happily. That was exactly what I needed to change my focus back to where it belongs, on my beautiful boys and not that rude doctor.

The rash has continued to get worse. Andrew has been throwing up and is clearly not feeling good, and this is becoming more common. We are worried, frustrated and of course exhausted as he is not sleeping well and so neither are we. My fears about GVHD continue to mount. But like a beautiful rainbow after a heavy storm, today we received a letter back from our donor, which was exactly what we needed after the last few weeks.

Dear parents of the recipient,

Thank you so much for your kind words. You asked how a twenty-four-year-old got on the marrow registry? Four years ago I took my then three-month-old little girl to one of her checkups at the hospital. They had set up a drive and asked if I would have my blood drawn and put on the registry. They said it was rare to be a match to a non-relative and I could always say no. Honestly, I took a bit of convincing as I had a small baby and my husband was deployed.

I had forgotten all about it when I received the call. I had even forgotten to tell my husband that I had signed up. When the call came I talked about it with my husband. We had concerns as we currently had a three-month-old in addition to our now four-and-a-half-year-old and three-year-old (all girls), but I couldn't say no, and my husband understood. At the time we had no information on the recipient. A few weeks into the process I found out it was a baby. My heart broke. A few friends tried to talk me out of it, as I was exclusively breast-feeding and would have to wean to a bottle. My response was, "My baby won't die because I give her a bottle, but another might." I weaned her and moved her from our bed to a crib, as we co-slept (made breast-feeding easier).

A few weeks before the donation I found out that they were able to do the collection locally. That made it so much easier. I only had to spend one night away from my family. The procedure went very well; one of the easiest they had ever done. I had no problems and was back to my family the next day. The only ill effect was it reduced my already fickle milk supply to nothing. Which is OK. My little one is now six months old and happily holding her own bottle. She is very close to daddy now too, which he loves. He was deployed the first year with the older girls, and is loving the baby stage he never witnessed before.

The process even helped me overcome my greatest fear: surgery, or general anesthesia to be specific. Even though I am a trained EMT, I had a hard time dealing with the idea as some relatives have had ill effects with anesthesia. I am happy to say that all went well and I no longer fear it. I think I would donate bone marrow again, actually.

I hope your little one recovers and lives a long, healthy, normal life. I'm a firm believer that everything happens for a reason even if that reason is very hard to see. My thoughts and prayers have been and continue to be with you all.

P.S. I have no objections to meeting some day. I hope that day will bring a smiling happy boy.

We are back in the hospital again. Andrew has developed a fever and is vomiting sporadically. His body is destroying his own platelets, and he has needed transfusions almost every day. It has been decided to finally do a skin biopsy to see if this rash is GVHD. I am not happy about putting my son through any more painful procedures, but the rash has been coming and going for far too long. We need to get to the bottom of it.

Thankfully, we have our own room, which is one of the perks of being less than a hundred days out from a bone marrow transplant.

"You are welcome to stay in here when we do this procedure, or you can step out — whatever you prefer," the doctor says. This dermatology resident doesn't know me and like most of the residents I come in contact with, she doesn't know our whole story. At this point, it would probably take a year just to read our file. So I try to be cordial with these residents, and even educate them a bit about HLH, knowing this might be the most they ever learn about it. I realize Andrew is just one of many patients she will see today, one of many sick children with a long, sad story, but somehow that doesn't provide me with any consolation, because this is my son and this is our sad story and it is real and painful — it is our lives.

"It's called a punch biopsy, and if you are staying in here you will need a mask, gown and gloves." She begins to assemble everything that will be needed: sterile instruments and towels, a small, special specimen cup to put the piece of his skin in, sterile gloves, a threaded needle and all the other stuff you need to cut a hole in someone's skin. Dressed in my gear, I sit down on our hospital bed, the only semi-comforting thing in the room, and hold my fourteen-month old baby in my arms as the doctor begins to clean the area on his leg that will soon be cut out.

Chapter 14

When the going gets tough, the tough get going.
—Joseph P. Kennedy

December 2008

*T*here it is, Cincinnati Children's Hospital; we finally made it and with twenty-five minutes to spare. We have just enough time to change our clothes in our car in the parking garage and get ready before our meeting.

"Do you have the notebook?"

"Yes. Can you imagine if I accidentally left it at home?" It has Andrew's whole medical life documented, charted and color-coded. "The hospital files have nothing on me," I say with a small smile. "Do you know where we're going?" I ask again, and Justin stops to look at me.

"Yes, I know where we are going. It's going to be OK," and he takes my hand as we step into the elevator.

I check my lipstick one last time and make sure my phone's ringer is off before the door quietly opens into the small exam room where we are waiting. Two doctors — a man and a woman — walk in, and Justin and I jump to our feet to shake hands and introduce ourselves. Knowing they are part of the expert team of HLH doctors, I suppose I have built them up in my mind. To what? I am not sure, but something other than what I saw, which was two normal people. They are about our age and that alone makes me think to myself, *how can they already be experts?* Our bone marrow coordinator is also in the room with us to take notes.

If I didn't know better, I would think everyone in the room could hear my heart beat. I breathe in deeply, hold it and let it out slowly, while correcting my poor posture.

"We are not sure if Dr. Edwards will be able to join us, so let's go ahead and get started. Even though we did receive Andrew's files from St. Louis, there is obviously quite a bit of history. We got through most of it, basically up through this past Labor Day when you learned his HLH was back again. If you wouldn't mind, go ahead and summarize the last three months," the doctor says.

"Well, let me begin by prefacing this all. It was Labor Day weekend, last year, when Andrew was diagnosed with HLH. I think it goes without saying that we thought a year later, this Labor Day, he would be on his way toward a full recovery. Sadly this Labor Day was nothing like we had dreamed of. We were back inpatient because Andrew was very sick. We spent the weekend getting even worse news than we expected. The HLH was somehow present in his body again, despite the bone marrow transplants.

"The last three months have been a nightmare; not that all of this hasn't, but this has been the worst. Andrew's health progressively declined. The roller coaster got faster and there has been no way to get off. After the news that his HLH was back our doctor started Andrew back on the HLH protocol. However, the prolonged steroid use finally caught up with him. Andrew's blood pressure became a huge problem and we struggled to get it under control. For a while we kept adding blood pressure medicines, one on top of the other. In addition, the rash got out of control. Andrew looked as if he had been dropped in a pot of boiling water. He was bright red and covered in blisters, he started to peel from the inside out. He itched nonstop and was inconsolable.

"After weeks of no improvement and my fight to convince everyone it was GVHD, I took matters into my own hands. I took a piece of butcher paper about ten feet long and hung it on the wall in our room. I listed his complete care for the last several months: drugs, tests, procedures, reactions and test results, desperate to try and pinpoint what was causing the rash. I still believed was GVHD, but since his two punch biopsies came back negative for GVHD, the doctors insisted it had to be a drug reaction. So we changed, substituted, deleted and added medicines, but it made no difference. We slathered topical steroid cream on him until he was so greasy it was hard to pick him up. I bathed him several times a day in Aveeno oatmeal baths, but nothing offered relief. In the midst of this, Andrew received his donor cell boost in mid-October. But before that could even start to work he developed several infections and we were back inpatient for quite some time. On top of that, Andrew went into adrenal crisis because his steroids were weaned too quickly, and he continued to combat dangerously high blood pressure until we finally had enough.

"I asked our nurse to let our doctor know I needed to speak to him, and it was urgent. This conversation was long overdue. After hours he finally walked in and did what he always did: took the stethoscope off the

IV pole, listened to Andrew, hung it back up and turned to walk out. But not this time. I point-blank asked him what was going on with my son.

"'What are we going to do? Is he dying? If he was your son, what would you do?' I couldn't sit in this room one more day and watch my son in pain, listen to him cry in agony, keep doing the same thing when it was not working. 'This is my baby. He has been to hell and back, and I am not going to just sit in here and let him die.'

"After a minute of silence he just looked at me, shrugged his shoulders and said, 'I don't know what to tell you.'

"That was when Justin and I decided it was time to contact you, the experts," I finish. "As we always say, 'if you keep doing what you've always done, you'll keep getting what you've always gotten.'"

"Well, clearly Andrew has been through more than his fair share, and we are sorry. We were hoping to see Andrew today, but we understand that since he just got out of the hospital yesterday, it would have been too much to try and drive here today with him. However, it is important that we do see him if you are interested in transferring your care here. Until then, we cannot say too much without examining him in person and running our own tests. The next step would be for you to come back with Andrew. In the meantime we can send you home with paperwork for your entire family to have labs drawn and sent here; that will give us much better information. Ultimately, it is your choice whether you transfer his care here. We are here to answer any and all of your questions in the meantime." Somewhere in the midst of my long-winded history report on Andrew, Dr. Edwards has joined us. I tried not to stare, but I was sitting in the same room as the world-renowned HLH expert. Justin and I are seeking a second opinion at another hospital, in another state that would require us to move in a last-ditch effort to save Andrew's life.

All three doctors begin to ask me specific questions, and thankfully, it is easy for me to find the exact answers because of my detailed record-keeping. I'm not sure how long this goes on because I'm so wrapped up in the conversation, but eventually things come to an end. As we stand up to leave, we thank them all repeatedly for their time, and Dr. Edwards leans in to give me a hug — a real hug, the first one I have ever received from a doctor. She very calmly and warmly says, "You have done a yeoman's job, Mom." I smile, as my mom is the only other person I have ever heard use that word, yeoman. I know at that moment she is the hope we are looking for, and Cincinnati is where we need to go.

Matthew holding his brand new baby brother

Andrew in the hospital before his offical diagnosis

Andrew's baptism on the rooftop garden

Andrew's first bone marrow transplant

Finally home together for Christmas

My precious boys: Matthew and Andrew

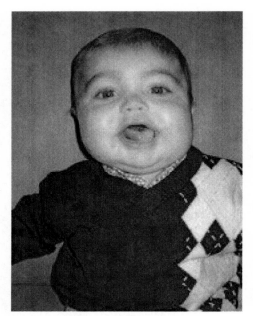

Our happy Andrew Bear

Andrew at home smiling for the camera

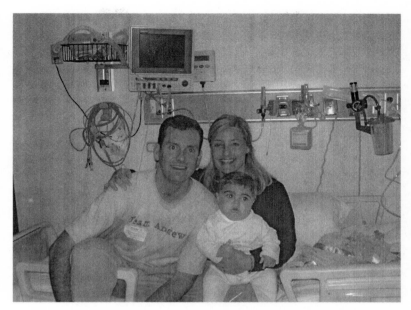

Andrew's second bone morrow transplant

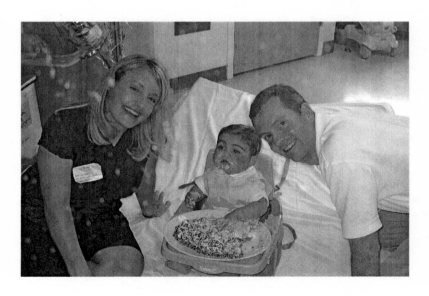

Celebrating Andrew's 1st birthday in the bone morrow unit

Our family - one of my favorite pictures

Beautiful brothers

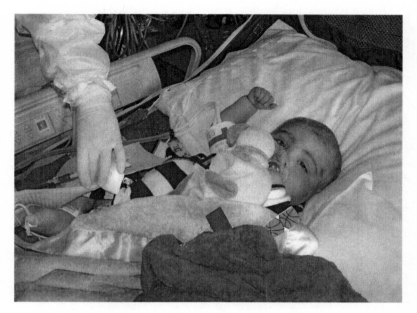

Andrew's thrid bone marrow transplant

Andrew and his fluffy brother Gilligan

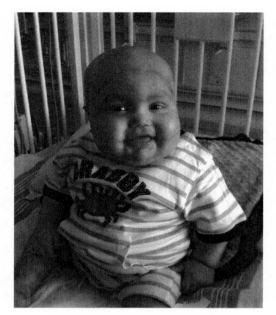

Our "crabby" son with his usual big smile

Our beautiful Matthew Man

Matthew on the first day of nursery school

Matthew the adventurer

Matthew enjoying life to the fullest

Matthew having fun at Six Flags

Matthew in the cockpit on our trip to Florida

Our last family picture weeks before Andrew died

Matthew's bone marrow transplant

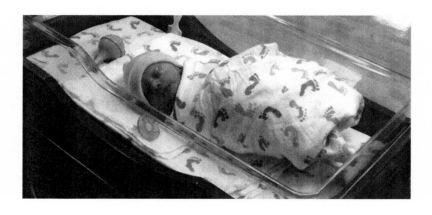

The first time we saw our son William

Our gift from above: William Clayton Akin

Chapter 15

Not everything that is faced can be changed.
But nothing can be changed until it is faced.
—James R. Baldwin

January 2009

*B*etween the ongoing bad weather in Cincinnati and St. Louis and the fact that Cincinnati Children's Hospital has been at capacity without a single available room, our transport day continues to get postponed. Justin and I have been discussing who should fly with Andrew on the medevac plane. I was not jumping at the chance to get on a plane the size of our minivan, but would have gladly done it for Andrew. However, we decided that since I have been inpatient with Andrew the last several weeks, Justin will go and get him settled in Cincinnati so I can go home for a night or two before I move up there indefinitely.

All eighteen months' worth of Andrew's files have been sent to Cincinnati Children's; I cannot imagine the pile of papers. There have been countless conversations between our bone marrow coordinator here and our new coordinator there to try to make sure everything is planned for. And then there are the medical plans that are needed to take Andrew on the plane. Cincinnati is sending their flight team and plane but our bone marrow coordinator from St. Louis will help because she is also a transport nurse. It gives me extra peace of mind that she is going. The doctors and the flight team have to discuss what machines, medicines and monitors he will need for the flight. My baby will be flying for the first time in his life on a medical plane; not exactly what I had in mind. But I am just thankful that Andrew will be given another chance. This flight will be taking him to Dr. Edwards and her team, and for that I am eternally grateful.

I pull out behind the ambulance and follow closely as we drive to the nearby airport. Luckily the airport is small and private, allowing me to pull up right next to the ambulance. Not fifty feet from where we are parked is the small propeller plane that will be taking my precious nineteen-month-old baby to Cincinnati Children's Hospital. The crew are dressed in special flight suits that make them look like a cross between an EMT and a fighter pilot. I go to Andrew, who lies strapped to the stretcher, all covered in blankets and hooked up to monitors. He has no idea what is going on, and I suppose that is one of the gifts of him being so young. Justin gives me a big hug and reassures me, as he always does.

"Go home and get some rest, and then you can drive up to Cincy. I will be with him the entire time and will call you once we arrive at the hospital." I know it is the right thing for me to go home and recharge for a few days, but I hate to leave Andrew for even a minute. I climb aboard the plane after he is loaded. I want to see it for myself. It is small. There is just enough room for Andrew's stretcher, which slides onto a built-in metal frame that fits securely on the one side, and a bench seat on the other side for the nurses, along with one seat for Justin. I know this is what the crew does for a living, Andrew is stable, and Justin is with him, but I just can't help but cry as we say our good-byes. The door shuts, and the plane slowly begins to taxi towards the runway. Justin waves to me from the tiny window until I cannot see him anymore, and then, just like a bird, the plane is off the ground and soaring into the clouds. I don't know how long I stand there after the plane is out of sight and the ambulance has driven away, alone with my thoughts.

Justin was right: going home is better than I could have imagined. It had been a while since I was home and walking in felt like I had just received a gift: the silence, the familiarity, the comforts — they are all there ready to greet me. The only thing about being home that could be better is if Matthew were here, but we decided he should be with family during this transition. After a long, hot shower, I get the call from Justin. They just landed in Cincinnati — that was fast. Our routine has always been I that stay inpatient with Andrew, and he stays home with Matthew so that he can work during the day and Matthew can attend school. But we usually switch on the weekends so I can see Matthew and he can see Andrew. This schedule has worked for us, for the most part. It is never easy to be away from each other and we both miss our other son, but we believe this is the best for the boys, considering the situation.

"Andrew slept during the entire flight and the ambulance was waiting to take us to the hospital as soon as we landed. It really was the smoothest flight I have ever been on," Justin said.

"Well, I am relieved and thankful it was uneventful and that you're there safe and sound. You were right, I needed to come home. I need to recharge my batteries, and there is no better place to do that than here."

"I'll tell you what, if we had any doubts about transferring Andrew's care, they were gone within minutes of our arrival. As soon as we came into our room in the bone marrow unit, the team was there to assess Andrew. Now don't freak out, just listen to me, Kristin. They found a very serious mistake. You know how you kept saying his blood pressure was just getting worse again, and he didn't seem to be responding anymore to his meds?"

"Yes," I say. "We kept having to spot him with more BP meds in between his regular doses because his pressures were so high."

"Well, that is because Andrew was receiving one of the wrong medicines. The doctors here figured it out. The good news is that what he was receiving is not life-threatening, but it's not blood pressure medicine and that's why his blood pressure was so high. Because of that mistake, his history of high blood pressure, and the fact that upon arrival his blood pressure was dangerously high, they don't want to sit on this. They have already consulted with the renal team and decided to transfer Andrew to the PICU. They want to put him on a blood pressure drip, and that can't be done in the bone marrow unit."

"OK," I say slowly.

"Kristin, I think this is a good thing. I know neither of us wants him in the PICU, but I am happy that the team is so aggressive."

"I agree. You're right. So do you want me to head up there right now?"

"No. I'll call you and keep you updated, but right now he is sleeping peacefully, so I think this will be a good thing. You just snuggle up with Gilligan tonight and get a good night's sleep. I love you."

They say that when you experience something traumatic in life, you are changed forever. Sometimes for the better and sometimes for the worse, but changed nonetheless. I agree completely. There are still many days that I say *hemophagocytic lymphohistiocytosis* out loud just to help me realize this is all really happening.

God, I am mad. Actually I am more than mad — I am furious! I know that life is not fair and that bad things happen to good people, but I am really struggling to make sense of what has happened to us. Some families leave their children alone for days in the hospital, some kids have nothing from home for

comfort and would rather stay inpatient than go home because it is safer. I see disgusting neglect, abuse of the system and lack of love, and yet so many of those kids survive.

I know it is not for me to judge, but how can I not? I feel like I am being punished. Andrew's diagnosis with a life-threatening disease, two failed bone marrow transplants, having to move to Cincinnati in a last-ditch effort to save his life, finding out that Matthew carries the same mutation as Andrew and will eventually get HLH, and the fact that they got the mutation from me. I just can't take any more. How do You expect me and Justin to keep going like this? How are we expected to continue to make life-and-death decisions for our children? Please, just spare my children. You can take me and punish me for eternity. I am yours — please just take me.

Chapter 16

Tough times never last, but tough people do.
—Robert H. Schuller

January 2009

he car is packed with all the necessities for living in a hospital room. Everything has been washed again just to be safe before being packed in huge ziplock bags. There is nothing left for me to do but leave. I walk back through the house one last time, not knowing when I will be back again. Thank God for my best friend Mel. She has agreed to drive up to Cincinnati with me, partly to keep me from falling asleep at the wheel but mostly to offer support. I don't know what I would have done without her throughout this ordeal. She has helped with Matthew more times than I can count. She visits me in the hospital, sends cards, brings meals, runs errands, and does anything I ask, happily and with a smile.

We have been best friends since we were twelve. Despite her having two younger sisters, I have always been known as the eldest sister in their family. And in my family she is my only sister — my only sibling for that matter, since I am an only child. I could not imagine my life without Mel. I have always joked that I never kept a diary because I have Mel. She knows everything there is to know about me and still loves me. So once we get on the road I don't even have to ask; I know she will be up for playing the state game. It is a standard for us on road trips: silly, but we seem to get amusement from it and it helps to pass the time.

We make good time and before I know it, I am pulling into the parking garage of Cincinnati Children's Hospital. I smell cigarette smoke as soon as we get out of the car. I see that people can't read any better here than they did at Children's. Of course there are no smoking signs everywhere, but for some reason, people feel the need to smoke in the parking garage — a space that already has poor ventilation. It really pisses me off. This is a children's hospital for God's sake! Mel and I fill our arms with as much as we can carry and begin to make our first of many trips to my new home, the bone marrow unit. We get buzzed into the unit, sign in and then head to Room 3. I slowly open the door and there in front of me is my Andrew Bear. He looks good! And he is already out of the PICU. Mel and I set down our first load of stuff and head back to the car for more.

I settle into our new home, unpacking and getting organized, something I have done many times now over the last year and a half. Even though I had seen a room in the unit before when we came for our initial consultation, I don't remember it being this small. There is very limited storage space but that's OK, I didn't bring much except the necessities: clothes, laptop, blankets and pillows, and toys for Andrew. I am definitely bummed out about the small window, not to mention our lack of a view. From our room we look onto a brick wall — yuk, plus I am only able to adjust the slats, not open the blinds up and down. It might sound like a small thing, but being able to have a view of something and see out makes a big difference day after day. But I didn't come here for the view. Mel stayed at a nearby hotel that first night before flying home the next day. I was sad to see her go.

Our doctor comes in to talk to us and before long my blood is boiling.

"Well, as you suspected, Mom, Andrew does have GVHD. Because it went undiagnosed for so long it is hard to say whether or not his body will respond to treatment. Before we can begin to prepare him for another transplant, we must get his GVHD under control." I listen as best I can, considering the news that just got dropped on me.

"We will begin treatment for his GVHD while also beginning the search process for a donor. Really at this point, we just need some time to see how Andrew responds."

How I wish we could turn back the clock. We wasted months and pumped so many toxic drugs into my baby's body to treat the wrong thing. When we first talked to Dr. Edwards after Andrew's initial diagnosis, we asked her whether we should stay in St. Louis or go to Cincinnati. All she could do was explain that based on the information we had provided, without seeing him, they would probably use the same HLH protocol as St. Louis. At that point Justin and I were just trying to keep up with all the new drugs and procedures. What we knew was that St. Louis Children's Hospital was a top-ranked hospital, it was in our backyard and we had no reason to think Andrew would not get the best care possible. But now, after being at Cincinnati Children's for just a few short weeks, I know that while the drugs are the same, that is the only thing that's the same. The level of care Andrew is receiving is not comparable. Everything is so different; each day continues to be an eye-opening experience, and now I know why going to the experts makes all the difference

It is hard to believe that I have already been living in Cincinnati Children's Hospital for a month and a half. Despite his PICU stay for high blood pressure, another line infection and treatment for chronic GVHD, Andrew bounced back, as he always does. Before long it was time to begin preparations for Andrew's third bone marrow transplant. It is the only way Andrew has a chance at being a long-term survivor. Shockingly, it rolls off my tongue with relative ease: *Andrew is going to have a third bone marrow transplant.* I remember our shock when we learned that his first transplant didn't work. A year and a half later we're so thankful that he is able to receive a third transplant. As Matthew often says, "I betcha didn't see that one coming." So we continue to do what we have done before: remain hopeful there will be another potential match on the registry who will be able and willing to try and save our son's life.

Every time I think we are making progress, something happens that seems to put us further behind than ever. That first month home after Andrew's second transplant I would have bet money that he was on his way to being a long-term survivor. But then one day things started to change, and it slowly progressed until we were back inpatient getting the news that his HLH was back again. And now we're in Cincinnati looking for a donor for his third transplant.

Meanwhile, we struggle with the next biggest decision of our lives: whether or not to take Matthew into transplant. We have another meeting scheduled to discuss this enormous decision. Our list of questions is long, and I have no doubt we will get them answered, but what they cannot do is make the ultimate decision. That's what I really need help with.

The nurse manager was not happy that Andrew won't sleep in a crib. She felt it was unsafe having him in bed with me because he could fall out. I tried to explain to her that since he first got sick at ten weeks, this is how we sleep together, but that did not calm her fears. I stood my ground, insisting that putting Andrew in a crib was not an option, so she offered to order us a special bed called a Posey bed. They often use them for little kids who are past crib age but could fall out of bed or have no adult supervision. I agreed to give it a try. As long as we can be together, that is all that matters.

The Posey bed looks like a giant Coleman tent. It is a metal frame that is connected to the perimeter of the hospital bed with a green mesh that encompasses the entire thing. The sides and end are white mesh that zip up and down. One day last week while Andrew was working with the physical therapist, I got creative. I decided to turn our Posey bed into a boat, the *Merry Marrow*, to be exact. I hit the playroom for some basic craft supplies and got busy. Soon the bed is decorated with nautical flags that spell out "Andrew," an anchor attached with rope, and a sign with our boat name and city of registration.

"It really looks pretty cute, if I do say so myself," I tell Justin on the phone that night.

"I am sure it does, Babe. I'm excited to see it when I'm up there next week. That's one of the things I love about you: you just being you. Making Andrew's hospital bed into a boat — you're always trying to find ways to make things special."

Sleeping in the Posey has been wonderful. Even though it makes our sleeping space a little smaller, Andrew seems to love it. Every night he laughs as I put my sleeping bag and my big pillow that we share in there. I make his bed right next to mine. With a few of his blankets it is almost like a little nest. He loves to snuggle in, holding a lovie in one hand and an extra pacifier in the other. We fall asleep together every night like this and I love it. I talk to him about our day and how much he is loved and cherished. He always reaches over and gently hits my face with his lovie, I think to make sure I am there, and of course it automatically makes me smile.

Yet despite this most treasured time together, I am still away from Matthew and that hurts. And worse, because of the flu restrictions that are set for the unit Matthew won't be able to see Andrew until late spring. I cannot put it into words, but Matthew and Andrew have a bond that surpasses brotherhood. From the day we brought Andrew home Matthew has been amazing with him. Now Matthew seems to see past Andrew's illness with its tubes and pumps. He has never complained about his brother being sick, about any of the modifications we have had to make — anything. There have never been any meltdowns or temper tantrums because of the amount of time I spend with Andrew. It is as if he understands all of this, as if he knows something the rest of us don't. He is loving, compassionate and completely selfless. He is my son and I could not be more proud.

Even though our nurses are used to the Posey bed and maneuvering within it to get vitals on Andrew and get access his line to change medicines is not a big deal, they don't allow Posey beds on transplant day. Having a tent over the bed would hinder access to Andrew in an emergency. I will miss our Posey. It has been a safe little hideout for Andrew and me. I can only imagine what it must look like with the nautical flags hanging above our heads and the two of us snuggled in with the sides all zipped up except for the small hole that lets the lines run from Andrew to his IV pole. I am confident everything will go smoothly today, as it has during Andrew's last two bone marrow transplants, and that we will be sailing on the *Merry Marrow* again in no time.

Getting to this day has been nothing short of a miracle. Andrew has overcome so many obstacles and complications in his short life; it seems whenever things start to go smoothly, the rug gets pulled out from underneath us, making us wonder what we are really standing on. Andrew's prep for this transplant was much more difficult than his first two because the drugs he received were stronger and dangerous. He had several serious reactions and that slowed things down. But despite everything, he keeps smiling, laughing and spreading love.

"It is amazing to think that these cells came from overseas!" I say. "The journey these cells have been on today is more than many people will take in a lifetime. I can only hope and pray that someday we will be able to take both boys to meet this donor and thank him personally." Our nurse begins to get things ready for Andrew's transplant. Overall things seem to be similar: again, he is hooked up to monitors to keep track of his vital signs as we start to infuse his new cells. He has been given all of his premedications and things are about to get started.

I try to take a picture but I am quickly reprimanded. The nurse manager tells me that by having a picture of the bag of cells I might be able to track down some information that could lead me to the donor, etc. At this point I am a lot more interested in documenting my son's third transplant than tracking down the donor, but I oblige. The nurse hooks the line up to Andrew, and Justin and I watch as what looks like blood but we know is something much more precious flows into Andrew's body. But this time Justin and I know that this is it. This is our last chance to save our son's life, and the excitement we felt before is tempered with fear.

Chapter 17

The hardest thing to see is what is in front of your eyes.

—Johann Wolfgang von Goethe

March 2009

We hear the knock and immediately jump to the door. We are exhausted but don't feel the full effects yet; we are too terrified to be tired. We are desperate to hear news, any news, because Andrew is somehow back in the PICU fighting for his life.

The new bone marrow cells were barely finished infusing yesterday when he started to go septic: vomiting and diarrhea, excessively high heart rate, low blood pressure and a fever. Justin and I jumped into our roles, working to clean and bathe Andrew as quickly as possible. Justin grabbed a washcloth, towel and clean clothes, while I filled the pink bucket with warm water and squirted Andrew's lavender bath soap in. Dr. Collins, the head of the bone marrow department, said in her thick British accent, "You two are like a synchronized swimming team," and we laughed for a moment. She was right; we are incredibly fortunate to have each other.

It was tense. The number of nurses and doctors continued to increase as Andrew proceeded to get worse. Andrew had gone septic before, but that didn't make the scene any less frightening. After several hours and everyone's best efforts Andrew was not stable enough to stay in the bone marrow unit, and sometime around midnight he was transferred to the PICU.

Justin and I stand shoulder to shoulder outside the door of Andrew's room in the PICU as the doctors begin to discuss our son's condition and their plans to save his life. While our nurse gives the report from the night, I scan everyone's faces to see if I can read their reactions.

"Mr. and Mrs. Akin, we are so very sorry. Andrew is a very sick little boy right now. He has bacteria growing in his blood and for someone with no white blood cells and no functioning immune system, this is life-threatening. As you know, Andrew went septic again this morning. His blood pressure plummeted and it was touch and go for a while. Right now,

Andrew is on five heavy-duty antibiotics to try and fight this infection; a pain medicine drip, which should help keep him comfortable; oxygen; and an inotrope, which will help raise his blood pressure. At this point, there is not much more we can do to support Andrew: we are giving him everything we have. Only time will tell if he can pull through this infection. We will just take it minute to minute." I make eye contact with each of the doctors as they finish rounds, but despite looking right at them, I cannot see their faces; it is as if I am looking right through them.

I don't realize they are finished speaking and have started to move to the next patient's room until Justin takes my hand to head back into Andrew's room. I walk to Andrew's bed and lean down near his face. I gently stroke his head and hold his hand while I quietly whisper in his ear, "Andrew it's your mommy. Daddy and I are here and we love you. We know how hard you have been working your whole life, and we could not be more proud of you. You truly are the most brave and courageous person we have ever known. We are so very sorry; we don't want to hurt you. We just want to help you, to save you, because we love you, but if you are too tired, if you are done, then please just give us a sign and we will let you go. But if you still want to fight, then show us; we will help you fight every step of the way."

According to *Merriam-Webster's Collegiate Dictionary*, a miracle is defined as: "1: an extraordinary event manifesting divine intervention in human affairs 2: an extremely outstanding or unusual event, thing, or accomplishment."

What has transpired over the last thirty-six hours is nothing short of a miracle. Yesterday morning, Justin and I stood at Andrew's bedside, holding each other and wondering if this would be the last day we would see our son alive. But by early evening Andrew had made a turnaround that stunned everyone in the unit. How could Andrew go from facing death to sitting up and holding his own bottle for the very first time? Obviously, it was a miracle. And I don't use that term lightly. The miracle was several things: early intervention by the doctor — she simply is outstanding; the quick response by the PICU team; but lastly, and most importantly, Andrew's endless will to live and his amazing spirit.

You know you have been living in the hospital a long time when it feels good to be back in the bone marrow unit. After three horrifying days in the PICU, we could not be happier to be back. Andrew isn't out of the woods, but this is a move in the right direction.

Just like at St. Louis, I have become close with many families here at Cincinnati Children's. While we are from all over the country and our lives back home vary greatly, in here we are all the same: scared parents fighting to save our children's lives. It doesn't matter what the disease or the treatment is, we speak the same lingo, we fight the same battles and we have the same fears. There is one mom that I have become especially close with: Lisa. Lisa is from Pennsylvania. Her son Brayton is a little younger than Andrew, but he also has HLH and has been sick most of his life, just like Andrew.

I am so thankful we met. I wish it was under different circumstances, but I can't imagine where I would be without her. We start every day by going down to the cafeteria for our coffee. We talk about our night, each understanding every word the other says. Lisa has been a tremendous support to me. We have made our sons friends, and they send each other cards and little gifts. Neither Andrew nor Brayton have had any friends before because they have spent their entire lives in the hospital. And it always seems that when Andrew is doing well, Brayton is not and vice versa. We talk a lot about our sons' disease: the issues, the fears, the complications. We cry and laugh and complain, but most of all we just do our best to make it through day after day. Lisa's friendship is a gift that I am eternally grateful for.

We have another meeting to discuss Matthew and our options. Our list of questions is so long now that it looks like a grocery list. We each take a seat at the small, round conference table. The room is only just large enough to hold a table and chairs, and a generic picture on the wall. Dr. Edwards begins. We listen intently but her language is so technical and scientific that we keep getting lost. I don't think she realizes how complicated these medical terms are, even when she explains something, but the beauty of Dr. E. is that she doesn't mind explaining it again until we do understand.

I repeat back what she has just told us. "So, even though Matthew is healthy right now, he carries the same mutation as Andrew. We won't know what or when, but we do know that it only takes one virus to trigger HLH. It could attack him as quickly and severely as Andrew, and he could be dead within twenty-four hours?"

"Yes, that is correct," she says gently. "I have discussed this situation with my colleagues several times, and we are all in agreement that the best option would be to take Matthew to transplant now."

I very calmly ask Dr. Edwards, "If this were your son, what would you do?"

"I would transplant him now."

That gives me some comfort, but not enough yet.

"He is perfectly healthy. It just doesn't make sense," I say.

"Either way, this is a very difficult situation and there is no easy or right answer. I'm sorry. Medically speaking, it makes more sense to take Matthew to transplant now as the odds are stacked in his favor: he's young; he's healthy and does not have the disease yet; there is a perfect match on the registry that may not be there when he needs it; and his exposure to viruses has been limited, since he is still so young. Not to mention the more obvious obstacles like taking him out of school and sports and spending time away from his friends. However, I understand the enormity of this decision, and I just want to help you in any way that I can. We don't want you two to feel pressured. Ultimately it is your choice."

What can we say? We thank Dr. Edwards for her time and leave the room, dumbfounded.

Heading back to the bone marrow unit, I feel like I am carrying the weight of the world on my shoulders. Justin and I walk hand in hand and don't say anything. We have just been told we need to take our healthy four-and-a-half-year-old into transplant. On our way back to the bone marrow unit we pass by the elevators that lead downstairs. Justin stops and pulls me towards them.

"Let's go to the cafeteria for a little while to talk this over; you know Andrew is in great hands with Nurse Amy." Riding the elevator down to the first floor I look at the other people and wonder, *did they just get the worst news of their lives, like us?* My eyes are filled with tears as I walk into the cafeteria. I grab some candy and a coffee, my staple in times of high stress, which is almost every day. We take a corner booth, trying for some privacy, if that is possible in a hospital cafeteria.

"I can't believe we are even considering putting Matthew through a bone marrow transplant," I say. "If Matthew had gotten sick as an infant and been diagnosed then, we would have learned about my mutation and I would never have had any more children. But no: Andrew gets sick and now we learn that Matthew will eventually get HLH and need a bone marrow transplant too. I just don't know how we can make such a life-altering decision. I understand all the reasons why we should do it now, but my heart says no. He is beautiful and full of life. If anything were to go wrong, I could never live with myself."

"Kristin, how can we not do it? You heard what Dr. Edwards said: there are all these reasons why it's better to do it now than to wait. Every other BMT doctor we've asked has said the same thing. How can we let him go back into the world, being a normal four-year-old boy, knowing that any virus could trigger HLH and he could be dead within days?"

I hear all of what Justin is saying, and I trust Dr. Edwards implicitly. But all of that aside, if God is real then where in the world is He? He would never expect me to make such a decision as this!

The more we talk about it, the more it hurts. The thought of putting Matthew through a bone marrow transplant seems almost surreal. Justin and I feel like we are damned if we do and damned if we don't. If we don't transplant him, how can he live a normal life, knowing that he is a walking time bomb? Yet if we do transplant him, the risks are big, and right now he is happy and healthy. Who are we to be making such incredibly huge decisions? Either way we will be stuck with wondering, "What if?" I don't see an easy answer and that infuriates me. And then there's trying to manage all the other logistics that go with this situation: Justin's job, our house, and everything else that gets put on hold when your child becomes critically ill. I feel like the weight of the world is on our shoulders right now and I don't see it changing any time soon.

But as we open the door to Andrew's room we are greeted with one of our favorite things: Andrew Bear, smiling, holding his lovie close to his face. He immediately sees us and throws his pacifier on the floor — his favorite thing to do. Justin and I start to laugh. How is that Andrew is always lifting our spirits when he is the one in the fight for his life?

Chapter 18

While you are upon the earth, enjoy the good things that are here.
—John Selden

Spring 2009

I lie in my sleeping bag all afternoon, cold, shivering, only getting out to turn up the heat in our room; willing myself not to be sick. If I get sick, who will stay with Andrew? He has never been without Justin or me. Besides, where am I going to go on Saturday night at 7 p.m., and how will I get there? Here in Cincinnati I don't have a car, I don't have any friends or family; my only friends are the nurses and other parents here in the bone marrow unit. Our nurse and I agreed today that if I wasn't feeling better by shift change I would leave. I thought maybe I was just worn down and extra-tired, but it is obvious I have a bug.

I see one of my favorite doctors standing in my doorway, and I know it is shift change time, 7 p.m., because this doctor only works nights. He is older and between his jovial personality and his looks, he reminds me of Santa Claus. I can always hear his laughter down the hall and when I do, it makes me smile. But I can see from the look on his face what he is about to say. With tears in my eyes, I grab a few things and rush out of our room. I know I can't risk making Andrew sick, if he hasn't already gotten whatever I have.

I know Andrew is in wonderful hands. I trust our nurses and know they are absolutely capable. Besides, he is sleeping and should be for the remainder of the night. But that's not the point. I don't leave my children. Everyone assures me he will be fine and that I can call to check on him throughout the night as they escort me out of the unit. The double doors shut behind me and I stand in the hallway alone, crying, trying to see through my tears. I am in my usual attire: a T-shirt, leggings and running shoes, holding my cell phone and a personal belongings bag from the hospital with a few necessities for the night away — I don't even know where that will be.

I dial Justin to let him know that he has to stop whatever he is doing, pack and make the six-hour drive to Cincinnati to be with Andrew. My sadness is quickly turning to frustration as I walk towards the elevator to leave the floor. I live in complete isolation; I spend over an hour a day wiping down everything in our room. I do it in the morning before our baths, in the afternoon and again at shift change. Many times in between I wipe down our door, the nurse server, the sink and the door handles. I even made a sign that covers our hand sanitizer, forcing everyone that enters to wash their hands with soap and water. How can I still get sick? I hate HLH.

Unfortunately, my parents are unavailable to take care of Matthew so he has to come along — not our first choice. I sit in the main corridor of the hospital trying to book myself a room at a nearby hotel. It is quiet. The hospital always feels pretty empty on the weekends. Several of our BMT nurses walk by as they leave for the night. They see me sitting in the lobby by myself.

"What are you doing? Why are you sitting here?"

"I'm sick and I'm trying to find a ride to my hotel room for the night."

"I'll take you," one of them offers.

"No, that's OK. If you get caught driving me you'll lose your job. It's not worth it. I'll call a cab."

"No," the nurse insists, "Just don't tell anyone."

"Seriously, I don't want to risk your job."

"Stop worrying. It will be fine." I stop crying about being sick and having to leave Andrew just long enough to say thank you, knowing the risk this nurse is willing to take on my behalf. It's not until I'm at the front desk of the hotel that I realize why the front desk clerk is looking at me strangely. I am dressed in what look like pajamas, my eyes are so swollen from crying they will barely open all the way and I'm holding a plastic bag with all my belongings. I don't bother to explain. He wouldn't understand and probably doesn't really care. I go upstairs to my room, take a long, hot shower and go to bed.

I awake to a loud knock on my door and look at the clock: two o'clock in the morning. I jump up, knowing that my sweet Matthew Man is just behind that door. He is half asleep in Justin's arms, but as he carries him in and lays him down on the bed, Matthew wakes up and realizes where he is. His face immediately lights up and he jumps into my arms. "Mommy!" I can't think of a better way to wake up at two in the morning. I kiss Justin good-bye and he leaves for the hospital to be with Andrew. Matthew and I snuggle in together and fall fast asleep — not before I can get a prayer in to feel better in the morning.

I wake up to Matthew squirming in our bed. I can tell he is awake and that makes me laugh. I don't feel much better but know I can't stay in bed today. Whenever Matthew comes to visit me in Cincinnati, I always try and plan adventures or "ventures" as he says, and while I wasn't planning on this visit, Matthew is here now and I will do my best to make it fun. As we get dressed I enjoy listening to him talk and ask me questions, just being his inquisitive self. We head out for pancakes, our favorite breakfast, and then hit the local Target for a few new trains. But the big "venture" is the Cincinnati Children's Museum. We arrive right when it opens, which is my best defense against germs and crowds. Within minutes Matthew has me climbing in tunnels and going down slides. I do my best, but I can feel a fever coming on, so we leave earlier than I would have liked. Walking out of the museum, hand in hand, Matthew excitedly asks me, "Mom, what ventures we going on next?" I am sorry to have to tell him that mommy is sick and I think that is all the ventures for today.

"How about we head back to the hotel, order pizza and watch movies?" It's not what I wanted and I know it's not what Matthew wanted. He doesn't complain or cry, because he just doesn't do that, but I can see he's disappointed, and that is way worse. It breaks my heart to let him down — to let both of my boys down. First I have to leave Andrew because I was sick and then I can't provide Matthew with the fun ventures he deserves. It surely can't get any worse.

I wake up in the morning feeling normal again. I'm so thankful — not because I cared about being sick; I just regretted the mess it caused my whole family. Matthew and I get up, check out of the hotel and head to the hospital for the changing of the guard. The floor of the parking garage we usually park on is full.

Matthew says, "Gosh, Mom, there are lots of cars here today. There must be lots of sick baby brothers."

"Yes, there are lots of sick children here — but they are getting better, just like Baby Andrew." As we approached the unit, Matthew says, "I would like to see Baby Andrew."

"I know, Buddy. He really wants to see you, but not quite yet." I don't even try to explain to him the restrictions that are imposed during flu season. He wouldn't understand and wouldn't care. It breaks my heart to keep him away from his brother, someone he has spent so little time with and yet loves so deeply. On the way into the hospital Matthew tells me he how excited he is about teaching his brother everything when he gets better.

His unending love and kindness for his brother are so amazing. So many siblings in this situation get mad at the sick one for getting all the attention and begin to act out, but not Matthew. He continues to love and cherish his brother more and more each day. I wish I could take credit for his attitude, but I know that it's just part of the magic that is Matthew.

As usual, Justin and I have no time to talk. We don't even stop to hug as we run by each other. Since Matthew can't come into the unit, he has to wait outside the double doors. Justin and I literally run past each other in the hall so that Matthew is only alone for a moment.

After a bone marrow transplant the doctors require you to stay near the hospital for several months. After Andrew's transplant at St. Louis Children's Hospital it was not a problem; since we lived in the same city, we were able to go home. But now that we are patients at Cincinnati Children's Hospital, we don't live in the same city. Where will we go when Andrew gets discharged? Between Andrew's long recovery from his third bone marrow transplant and the possibility of Matthew having a transplant as well, we will be in Cincinnati for a while. There are really only two options: the Ronald McDonald House or a furnished apartment.

The Ronald McDonald House, which is right next to the hospital, is a great option for most families, but for kids with compromised immune systems it is not ideal. Justin has spent a lot of time researching furnished apartments in the Cincinnati area, looking for something big enough for all four of us that allows dogs. It needs to be near the hospital, since we will still be there several days a week for clinic visits. Ideally, the complex will be near a grocery store, etc., and it has to be fully furnished. This is a long list of must-haves but if anyone can find it, Justin can.

And as promised, we finally get our new home sweet home. I am excited about moving in — finally, we have a place where we can all be together again. Andrew will be spending his second Easter in the hospital, this time with Daddy, while Matthew and I break in the new apartment. And you better believe I will have plenty of super fun ventures lined up for us.

Finally, after months and months of living apart, we are all together under one roof and it feels awesome. The apartment Justin found is perfect. Of course it has all the basic necessities of home: our own washer and dryer, two bedrooms, two bathrooms, and it's completely stocked with everything from dishes to a vacuum cleaner. We don't have to worry about bringing anything from home other than clothes and toys, which takes a tremendous load off our shoulders. But I cannot adequately explain the most important thing it means to us: privacy, freedom and time with all of us together. This apartment allows us to make memories and just be a family.

What an unexpected but much-needed surprise! Justin has planned a trip to Florida for just Matthew and me. It is as if he can read my mind.

"I know that you guys need some special bonding time. Matthew and I have already gotten to do so much over the last year and a half while you and Andrew have been in the hospital," he says. I am moved to tears.

"Thank you . . ." is all I can muster as I wrap my arms around my husband to hug him. In addition to all the fun trips they have been on together, Justin and Matthew have also had lots of time together at home, just being father and son. Of course I don't begrudge him any of that special time, but I am envious, because I miss Matthew as much as he misses Andrew. This trip will be a wonderful opportunity for Matthew and me to have one-on-one time, get away from the hospital and just have fun at the beach!

Chapter 19

Life shrinks or expands in proportion to one's courage.

—Anaïs Nin

June 2009

*S*omehow — and I am not sure how — our bad luck streak seems to continue. Matthew is sick again; he has a fever and is throwing up. He lies on the couch in our new apartment, listlessly watching cartoons with a cool rag on this forehead while Justin and I talk over the phone about what to do. The question is, will this bug be gone in the next twenty-four hours or will it linger? Of course neither of us knows. I hate to stay home and miss our trip if he will be back to his old self by tomorrow, but I also hate to push him when he is clearly sick. And what if he gets worse before he gets better?

I suppose this decision wouldn't be so tough if the last two years hadn't been filled with so many hard decisions, but this seems to be the straw that breaks the camel's back. We are scheduled to fly out early tomorrow morning but we still have to make the drive to Louisville from Cincinnati and that means we have to decide now.

I have talked up this Florida trip every day since Justin first told me about it. I just want to take Matthew to the beach for a few days, to be able to play in the sun and the ocean, and to be completely away from disease, medicine and hospitals. Is that asking too much? After weighing the pros and cons, we decide to go for it. I load the car and try to make Matthew as comfortable as possible with a pillow behind his head and his train quilt on his lap. I can tell he doesn't feel well, but you would hardly know it because as usual, he just doesn't complain.

The drive goes smoothly and we check in our hotel near the airport by late afternoon. However, as the hours pass into the evening Matthew is not getting better. He seems to be just as sick as when he woke up this morning.

"Babe, I'm sorry to keep calling you, but if we are going to make the flight, then I'm going to have to wake Matthew up now."

"I know he had a bad night but I still think you guys should try and go. Hopefully by tomorrow he will be better, and I would hate for you to have missed this trip together."

"I agree. I just hate this. The good news is Matthew's fever is gone so hopefully the rest of this bug will be soon. Take good care of Andrew Bear and give him lots of kisses from us. We love you."

The weather could not be more perfect: sunny, bright blue skies and cool breezes blowing through the beautiful palm trees. Our hotel is great — right across the street from the beach. Justin took care of every detail, as he always does. We spend many hours at the beach, playing, digging and just running around. Watching Matthew make friends every day with whatever kids are on the beach is priceless. Matthew is social and friendly, and he just makes fun wherever he goes. My pride beams off me like the sun off the water. In addition to the beach, we head out for some fun ventures. We use the water taxi to get around, which is fun all in itself, and we find the local children's museum, which Matthew loves.

While Matthew and I soak up all that the beautiful Florida coast has to offer, Justin is back in Cincinnati trying to get settled with Andrew in the apartment. They just got discharged, and while you would think that is good news, Andrew's home care responsibilities have grown so much that it is almost more than Justin can handle. I can hear the frustration in Justin's voice every day when we call to check in, and I feel bad. But today I can hear he is on the verge of tears.

"He's hardly sleeping, and I can barely keep up with all his medicines. He has something due almost every hour around the clock, and to top it off, he is stooling non-stop."

"Honey, we can come home early," I offer, but I know he won't let us.

"No way. You and Matthew need this time together. I'll manage."

I am making the most of every second: the sun, the breeze, the beauty — but most of all, the time with Matthew. I am trying to be fun and do everything that he wants, but I know inside that Matthew wants his daddy there too, and so do I.

Justin was not exaggerating about Andrew's home care. He has so many medicines I have typed up a schedule and keep it on a clipboard so we don't miss anything. If I am not taking one medicine out of the fridge an hour before it is due then I am making his anti-fungal medicine, doing a sterile dressing change or taking his blood pressure one of four times a day. He is hooked up to at least one pump twenty-four hours a day and many hours it is two pumps. It is a gigantic responsibility and we cannot make a mistake. But thankfully, he is still being seen in the clinic and day hospital most days of the week so I know there are several sets of eyes monitoring his labs and overall condition.

Lying in my twin bed, I look over to see my Andrew Bear sound asleep in his twin bed. I get up and quietly peek into the other bedroom to see Justin and Matthew soundly sleeping too. Gilligan hears me and comes to join me on the couch in the family room. Today is Andrew's second birthday. So much has transpired in the last year that it is almost impossible to believe. And while we're not where we hoped we would be, we could not be more grateful that we are all together to celebrate this monumental day that many times we thought we would never see. Before long I hear Matthew talking in the other room. Soon everyone will be up and we can begin celebrating Andrew's second birthday.

Watching Matthew help his baby brother open presents is a gift all unto itself. The love between our two sons is amazing. He is gentle, as if he truly understands his brother's condition. Andrew is just happy to have his big brother right next to him. He keeps touching him and laughing. Matthew is keeping busy showing Baby Andrew how all his new toys work, while I get the cake ready with the candles. Justin straps Andrew into his little booster seat and Matthew is running around in excitement. We all chime in together to sing "Happy Birthday," while Andrew smiles from ear to ear. He's unsure what to do with his cake until I show him that he can touch it, and then he immediately digs in. I am not sure who is enjoying this more; us watching him eat, or him eating. Andrew is covered with blue and green icing — it's all over his chubby little cheeks, as well as his hands and clothes. Clearly he loves it, and we love that he is so happy. This is what birthdays are all about.

Every time, every *single* time Andrew starts to make progress, and I mean the smallest baby steps, for which we give huge thanks, something rare and unexpected comes along and throws us off course. The last forty-eight hours have gone from bad to worse — and fast. Little did I know that two days ago when we came into the clinic for labs we would wind up in the PICU again, hoping and praying yet again that Andrew is going to make it.

No matter how many times you have seen your child fighting for his life, it never gets any easier or less terrifying. It all happened so fast. One minute we were sitting in our room waiting for the nurse to come in, and the next minute Andrew and I were covered in blood. I had begun to change his diaper and as soon as I opened it up, I was shocked to find the entire diaper full of blood and blood clots. I couldn't figure out where it was coming from, but it continued, and I called for the nurse in a panic. The doors flew open, bright lights switched on and our room began buzzing with people. Andrew's blood pressure was dropping and it was obvious that we were headed for the PICU.

I am comfortable — or perhaps I should say it feels familiar — sitting in the PICU. Our previous experiences in the PICU have taken some of the edge off, but I hate it that much more because of our past history. I don't want to know this unit, I don't want to know so many of the nurses, I don't want to know that the orange name tag I must wear around my neck denotes to all who see me that my child is in the dreaded PICU.

The cause of the bleeding remains unknown, so Andrew is taken into surgery to try and find out more. I sign the papers without looking at them; I have it done it so many times, and there is no time to argue anyway. They think he might be bleeding internally, maybe from an ulcer or GVHD of the gut. The upper and lower colonoscopy should provide the information that is needed, and of course, if he is bleeding internally, then they will cut him open.

I go and sit in the OR waiting room, as I have done so many times before. I can't watch TV or read a magazine, so I just walk, because sitting still is impossible and I feel as if I will jump out of my own skin. And sadly, I am alone because Justin and Matthew are in Austin for a family reunion. This sucks!

"Justin, you need to sit down for this," I say. "It is confusing and overwhelming and a whole new set of problems. The initial bleeding in his diaper the other day in clinic was from a cyst that burst. However, it was during the upper and lower endoscopy that the doctors determined that Andrew has a more serious problem than originally thought. Andrew has a severe case of pneumatosis."

"What does that mean? Like pneumonia?" Justin asks.

"No, it's not pneumonia. It is gas-containing cysts on the wall of his intestines. They told me it is fairly common in BMT patients because of the prolonged use of steroids and chemotherapy, both of which cause inflammation. However, what is not as common is for one of the cysts to burst, which is what initially caused all the bleeding from Andrew's rectum. And the follow-up X-rays that were done after surgery showed even more bad news: Andrew's intestines and the surrounding area are full of air." I pause to choke back tears. It is quiet on the other end as well.

"Babe? Are you still there?" I ask.

"Yes," Justin says slowly.

"They told me this additional issue is extremely dangerous, so Andrew has been started on three new antibiotics. I didn't think there were any left he wasn't on since his transplant. At this point the biggest concern is internal bleeding, so he'll continue to have X-rays every six hours to monitor the situation. If he starts bleeding internally they'll take him back into emergency surgery." I'm crying now. "And if all this wasn't enough, he hasn't had anything to eat or drink in over ten hours. I've just been told that he can't have anything by mouth until further notice because of the risk it poses to his GI system. He is being started on TPN and lipids, so his gut will have a break. Andrew has screamed to the point where his voice is almost gone. He keeps pushing me out of bed towards his stroller because he knows his milk is in there, but I can't give it to him!

"I can't stand this anymore! I don't understand why he can't just get better. Why does every rare and odd thing keep happening to him? What I wouldn't do to be able to trade places with him, to let him be healthy and me be sick!"

"Listen, Kristin," Justin says. "I am going to leave Matthew here in Dallas with my mom and I'll be on the next flight to Cincinnati. Just hang in there. Don't give up."

"I'm not, I just know his body can't keep going like this forever."

"I know, but Andrew is strong and he is going to make it," Justin says forcefully.

"I know, I just can't stand to see him suffer another second."

I sit on the end of Andrew's bed and let out a huge sigh. He is finally sleeping peacefully, something he desperately needs. The doctor and I almost came to blows earlier about what pain medicine to use. I told her over and over what works for Andrew. I even showed her my notes, but for some reason she just dismissed me.

"OK, I have been by Andrew's side every day of his life and documented everything," I ended up saying. "I am not a doctor, but I do know my son better than anyone else, and he has been to hell and back more times than I care to count. You are not in this room around the clock listening to his screams, and because of that you really don't get it. I am not asking anymore, I am telling you: we will get Andrew's pain under control today — period." I could feel the tension I had created, but I didn't care.

I watch our nurse hang his new bag of liquid nutrition (TPN and lipids), and I honestly can't believe that all the pumps hooked onto his IV pole even fit. Like the overloaded IV pole, my brain is at the point where it just can't take on any more stress, anxiety or fear. I think somehow part of your brain just shuts off — at least mine does. Actually I think it hibernates; if I were truly able to comprehend all the pain and suffering my son has had to endure, I would go crazy.

We have settled back into our routine here in the PICU. All of our worldly possessions are in a bag on the floor under the bathroom sink. Our laptops are the only things we keep nearby. Justin sleeps on the pull-out chair/bed and I sleep with Andrew, as usual. The rooms are new, clean and relatively spacious, with a machine that comes down from the ceiling and surrounds the bed for everything to hook up to. It looks a little futuristic, but you quickly learn to look past all that and only see what matters: your child in the bed. Quiet time is hard to come by in here; our nurse is in and out of the room almost nonstop.

And Andrew is very sick. We take turns going down to the cafeteria, mostly to get a break from the room. I can feel the eyes on my orange name tag — anyone who has spent time in this hospital knows about the orange tag. But in some strange way, it almost feels like a badge of courage, like you want people to know that your child is fighting for his life and that whatever they are dealing with is probably not that bad.

Coming back to the unit, you have to show your badge to get buzzed in. You never know what you're going to find when you come into the small waiting room that leads to the elevators. It's often filled with family and friends of patients that have just had a severe trauma, gathered at the hospital waiting to hear more. There are times when I pass through when I can tell the family is here to say their final good-byes. We have even had the unit on lockdown, because a gang member was in and there were concerns that a rival gang member would try and come to finish him off. As if my own son's battle was not enough.

Just as we are getting used to some quiet days, Andrew begins having frequent vomiting episodes. But instead of normal vomit, there is something different and alarming about what is coming up. It is the dark brown of old blood and stomach bile. The PICU team immediately consults with the

GI team, who say it is common for this to happen for the first few days after an endoscopy. But instead of stopping, the vomiting is getting worse. No wonder Andrew needs so much pain medicine; what comes out looks like dark green swamp water and there is no way that can feel good in his stomach. It is the strangest thing: Andrew will be sleeping peacefully and then wake up, crying and fussing until suddenly the vomit comes. Then, after he is cleaned up, he peacefully goes back to sleep. It is almost as if he is possessed. The additional X-rays and ultrasounds have not given us any idea about what is causing this ongoing vomiting, so he is scheduled for a CT. This test requires Andrew to have an NG tube placed through his nose and into his stomach, a peripheral IV for the contrast dye, transport down to the CT and sedation to keep him still during the test. We just can't win for losing.

"Mrs. Akin, can you step out for a minute?" I look up and see a few doctors, but can't even remember what group they are from; surgery, anesthesia, GI, PICU — my mind has gone numb.

"The CT scan results have given us more information, and I am sorry to tell you, but Andrew has a duodenal hematoma. This is a separate issue from the pneumatosis caused by the upper and lower endoscopy done on Monday. It is very rare that this happens, but it happens nonetheless. I am so sorry. The good news, however, is we don't feel that it is necessary to open Andrew up this time. He will need to have another NG placed with ongoing suction to help keep his stomach empty until the hematoma can heal. That, of course, just takes more time," the doctor explained.

"Like how much more time?" I ask, concerned.

"At least several more weeks," he says.

"Let me get this straight: Andrew won't be allowed to eat or drink for weeks? He will continue to receive liquid nutrition, all the while being connected to something on the wall that is pulling sludge from his tummy? OK, I have heard enough," I say calmly. To say I feel defeated right now would be an understatement.

Even though I didn't want to put Andrew through another thing, I knew this NG tube should help him feel better. But I had no idea it would help so quickly. The nurse usually listens with her stethoscope to make sure the tube is in the right spot within the stomach, but that was not necessary today, because dark green sludge immediately started flowing out of the tube into the container on the wall. In no time it was full and had to be dumped. Seeing that come out of my baby's tummy via a tube up his nose was devastating, but as disgusting as it was to see, it made me feel better as it continued to pour out. *That must be giving him some relief,* I think.

Although the NG tube is doing its job, Andrew is not happy about having a tube up his nose and is going crazy trying to pull it out. Try explaining to your two-year-old that he mustn't touch the highly annoying tube in his nose. Initially, I tried to sit in bed with him and hold his hands, but that was not going to be the answer. Our nurse insisted we put arm restraints on Andrew to keep from pulling the tube out of his nose. The arm restraints almost put me over the edge. My sweet Andrew Bear is going crazy because we just took away his ability to soothe himself. He always has a pacifier in his mouth and another one in his hand, not to mention a lovie in the other hand and I think not having the use of his hands is harder for him than the NG tube. I have to talk to the doctors about possible sedation options, or anything to make Andrew more comfortable and help him through this.

First pneumatosis, now a duodenal hematoma. I have to step back and ask, what are the chances of all this happening?

Well, in our case, pretty good I suppose. If HLH occurs in 1.2 out of every million newborn children, and Andrew has undergone not one, not two, but three transplants, again with a probability so low it's off the charts, and has a genetic mutation of which less than a hundred cases have been documented in the world, then I suppose having pneumatosis and a duodenal hematoma is not that odd.

And on top of this, Matthew will be starting his pre-transplant workup in the next two weeks so he can have a bone marrow transplant. I don't know what situation is worse right now, but I do know that Justin and I are overwhelmed with pain, bad news, and exhaustion from this two-year fight to save our sons.

Chapter 20

Strength is a matter of a made up mind.

— John Beecher

Summer 2009

*F*inally, after several weeks inpatient, Andrew's hematoma healed and we got to go home. All five of us just living together, loving each other and giving thanks for all we have. As the clock ticks and Andrew continues to get further out from his third transplant, we are getting that much closer to starting Matthew's transplant. I am not sure whether it is fate, coincidence, or just plain bad luck, but Matthew will be checking into the bone marrow unit two years to the day after Andrew first went to the hospital and this nightmare began.

I am trying to soak up every moment of our priceless time together and store it all inside me for the days ahead when I know I will need it. We have so much to be grateful for: Andrew is finally 100% engrafted after having two failed bone marrow transplants; his blood pressure is currently under control, allowing us to wean him off his blood pressure meds; and most importantly, he is home with all of us in the apartment. He is even starting to regain his strength and is beginning to try and pull up and stand. While Andrew has not yet walked, I know in time he will. His struggle for health has taken everything his body has got, so walking and talking will come in time; I have no doubt. For the first time in a long time, it really feels like Andrew is going to make it. He is going to beat HLH; he will be what we call a long-term survivor. And we are especially thankful that Andrew is doing so well as we prepare for Matthew's journey.

There could not have been a more difficult decision than going ahead with Matthew's bone marrow transplant. Justin and I have stewed about this, argued about it and cried about it. More than anything we have struggled with sheer disbelief since we first received the news more than seven months ago that Matthew also has the gene for HLH. After count-less hours of research, several meetings with our doctors and discussions with other BMT parents, we finally made the decision to go ahead, and we can only hope and pray that it is the right one. God knows it was made out of love and out of our desire to give our son the best chance of survival.

Even though Matthew is healthy and does not have HLH like his brother did, he still has to undergo all the same pre-transplant tests: countless labs; pulmonary function test; bronchoscopy and endoscopy; EKG; echocardiogram; bone marrow aspiration and biopsy; glomerular filtration rate; X-rays; CT scans; and MRI's. I am more than familiar with all these tests, since Andrew has had them all several times, but of course Matthew never has. He has never undergone general anesthesia, he has not had a critical, life-threatening illness, and he feels fine, so it is difficult to try and explain why we're putting him through this.

Until now we have chosen not to say anything about his upcoming transplant. We felt there was no reason to scare him, especially when he has no real concept of time. Justin and I wanted him to have as much fun this summer as possible, but now that time is over and we are staring straight into beginning our fourth bone marrow transplant in less than two years! Try explaining to your four-and-a-half-year-old that getting a central line will be a good thing because he won't have to have so many pokeys (needles).

As we sit Matthew down to try and explain what is about to take place, it takes all I have not to just break down and hold him in my arms. Instead I try desperately to put a simple, kid-level twist to it.

"Matthew, remember how you had all those pokeys and the nurses took some of your blood?" I ask calmly. "Well, the doctors found a yucky bug in there and we need to get it out before it makes you very sick." He looks at me, somewhat confused, as I proceed. "So that's why you've been having so many tests lately: to look inside you and see exactly where the bug is. To get this bug out we'll have to stay in the hospital for a while, and you will get some medicines that should get rid of the bug. You might have days that you don't feel good, but we have medicine to help with that. We'll be staying in the bone marrow unit, the same area Baby Andrew was in. I will stay with you in the hospital the entire time, and Daddy will be in the apartment with Baby Andrew. We'll bring games and toys from home, and we can even bring our Wii. Does that make sense? Do you understand?"

"Yes, Mommy. I understand. I remember one time when I was at Charlie's grandma's house and I fell down and scraped my knee. That must be when the bug got inside me."

"Oh, Matthew, honey," I say with a smile, with tears filling my eyes, "Yes, you're right. Maybe that's when the bug got in." Justin and I decide not to tell Matthew about his hair loss yet. We don't want to scare him. Instead, Justin decides that the two of them will both get buzz cuts, so it will be less traumatic when his hair does fall out — if that's possible. What an awesome dad!

I am overwhelmed at the sweetness and gentle nature of my son. Already, taking him through these tests has been a test of my deepest strength. It was different with Andrew because every step of the way, there was no choice. He was always sick, fighting for his life. Looking into Matthew's crystal-blue eyes and thinking about what lies ahead is like sticking a knife into my heart. I could never have imagined the love I would feel for these two little boys; being their mom really is indescribable. I love them more than anything or anyone and would go to the ends of the earth for them. To see them suffer is slowly killing me, little by little, day after day.

Checking into the bone marrow unit is easy. It is my second time in less than a year here at Cincinnati Children's Hospital and my fourth time in less than two years. I think I have earned the equivalent of an undergraduate degree in bone marrow transplant life. I have gotten to be a master at packing and unpacking, setting up our home away from home in the small rooms. After making the Merry Marrow for Andrew my creative juices were already flowing, so I immediately turned our room into Matthew's Marrow Train, complete with a huge train on the wall, special shirts for his transplant day — the works. But all of that is secondary to the one and only thing I really care about, and that is lying in bed next to Matthew. While it is a tight fit, he insists that I sleep with him or "snuggle bunny" as he calls it, and I wouldn't have it any other way. We lie in our sleeping bags, he in his cute blue and white gingham puppy dog bag monogrammed with his name, and me in my North Face bag. I have managed to fit quite well on my side with my head leaning into the upper bed rail while my lower half is held in the bed by the lower bed rail. Our heads touch and I can't stop telling him how proud we are of him, how much we love him and how strong he is.

Meanwhile, Justin is living in our apartment with Andrew and keeping busy around the clock. They are at the hospital several days a week for labs and infusions, so I get to see Andrew then and Justin stops by to see

Matthew. So far Matthew seems to be tolerating the chemo well, but it is still early; we are only a few days into our almost two-week regimen.

Matthew looks and feels good, but I know it is only a matter of time before it catches up to him. For now, my biggest challenge is keeping him entertained in this tiny room. We have a daily routine, and we have lots of fun things to help the time go by, like watching Scooby-Doo — our new favorite — reading books, making crafts and playing Wii.

We even have our child life therapist set up a special private play time just for Matthew and me in the play room so he could get out of his room and play Guitar Hero. I was so excited for him and thought he would love it, but as we enter the play room, Matthew just looks around and says, "Mom, where are all the other little boys? Can't someone come in and play with me?" I try to explain that for now we have to be extra careful about germs and that he can't be around anyone else besides me and Daddy until we get rid of the bug, but it breaks my heart and clearly his too.

He can't stop talking about his best friend, Charlie, and how they are super spies. He keeps telling me and anyone who comes in our room that when he gets home he and Charlie are going to dig their way to China and make a secret club with no girls allowed, except for me. The day that he and Charlie are playing together again cannot come soon enough for him or me.

This past year Matthew was in his second year of nursery school, and boy, did he love it. The first year he was in the "yellow room," which he enjoyed, but halfway through the year we pulled him out because of our fear of infection. It was only about six months after Andrew had been diagnosed with HLH, and we were terrified. However, we realized that Matthew needs and wants to go to school, so when fall came around we let him go back to school, this year in the "blue room."

The blue room is what parents dream of for their child's nursery school experience. It's the perfect combination of play, structure and love, with the most loving and nurturing teachers. Matthew loves his teachers and we love them too! He loves his friends and every day he would happily run in to school. I will never forget his first day of school. I walked him in, stopping to get several pictures in front of his school sign. He looked like a little prince and I was smiling from ear to ear. We walked in, he hung up his backpack, and without so much as a pause, Matthew walked towards the other kids and started to play with them. He is brave, he is adventurous, and he knows no fear. I could feel the pride bursting out of my chest. Wow-how did I ever get so lucky to have him for my son?

Chapter 21

We could never learn to be brave and patient
if there were only joy in the world.
—Helen Keller

August 22, 2009

Sometimes people just don't get it. Actually, most people don't get it and I get that, I really do. I know it's hard to imagine what it is really like living in here. Most of our friends and family still can't say the name of Andrew's disease, and many people still get it confused with cancer. There are so many things about my life that have changed I can barely remember life before all of this.

My reference point is so different now I rarely realize how far from normal we really are, but this is what our reality looks like:

- 11:00pm - House cleaning comes in and empties the trash in room and bathroom
- 11:30pm - Linen man comes in to get the linen cart and hang a new bag
- 12:00am - Vitals-I always get up and help with his vitals, I do his blood pressure because we have our own electric cuff, plus I change his diaper, weigh it and mark it down
- 12:30am - Nurse comes in to start antibiotic
- 1:00am - Pump beeps done with antibiotic, I get up and silence it, call for the nurse and she comes in and hangs the flush
- 3:00am - Nurse comes in to hang another med
- 3:15am - Pump beeps done with med, I get up and silence it, call for the nurse and she comes in to hang flush
- 3:45am - Nurse comes in to draw 4am labs and get vitals-getting labs is always tricky, Andrew's line is positional, I know where to push on his chest to get it to draw, change his diaper and finally around
- 4:15am - get him back to sleep
- 4:30am - I head back to bed
- 5:30am - Nurse comes in to hang antibiotic

- 6:00am - Pump beeps done with med, I get up and silence it, call for nurse and she comes in to hang flush
- 6:30am - Nurse comes in to hang another med
- 7:30am - House keeping comes in to get trash
- 8:30am - Pump beeps done with med, plus nurse is in here to do morning assessment and vitals; I get Andrew's stuff ready for his bath
- 8:45am - PCA comes in with baby scale to weigh Andrew and brings clean linens
- 9:00am - Nurse comes in to hang 2 meds; I give Andrew his bath, change his linens and give him any oral meds due for the morning
- 9:30am - Doctors knock on the door for rounds-I come out and join them and then they come in to see Andrew
- 10:00am - I take a shower 10:20am - CVC nurse comes in to check Andrew's dressing and central line site
- 10:45am - Staff member comes in to check supplies of nurse server
- 11:00am - Nurse comes in to give me another oral med to give Andrew
- 11:30am - Different doctor stops by to check on Andrew, child life stops by to see if we need any new toys
- 12:00pm - PCA comes in to do vitals and check room supplies
- 1:00pm - Nurse comes in to hang 2 meds
- 1:15pm - Pump beeps, I silence it and call for nurse, she comes in and hangs a flush
- 2:00pm - Hang another med

As you can see, there is a lot going on and this is a quiet stay-meaning Andrew is not critically ill like he has been in the past. He is also on very few meds-which cuts down on the nurses coming in. In addition, none of the meds he is getting right now require heart leads but when he is on that monitor it beeps off and on based on his numbers. I sleep in a sleeping bag on the pull out bed/chair because it is easy to get in and out of and zip back up. Food-when Justin is in town he usually brings me something otherwise I get something from the cafeteria and bring it up. I am able to use the bathroom in this room which is a blessing-I will not be able to with Matthew. The rule is-if the patient is using the bathroom the parents may not. Therefore, I will have to go down the hall and into the parent lounge just to go to the bathroom. In the meantime, the pumps will sometimes beep for silly reasons-air in the line or down occlusion-thus requiring the nurse to come in again. I did not even mention, PT, OT and Speech therapy that comes by every day or so. Plus, the dietician follows up closely as well and the Chaplain stops in regularly. As you can see, it is a revolving door. There is hardly any quiet or down time. I try and sleep during the day when Andrew sleeps since I don't get much at night. I was surprised when I was home last that a few friends and neighbors still did not understand that when Andrew is in patient-we *Do Not Leave Him-At All!* Whether it is Justin or me-we are with him 24 hours a day. This room is our home.

The reality is this: Matthew is five days away from receiving his new bone marrow cells. He is undergoing the same harsh chemotherapy regimen that Andrew received with his third transplant. Matthew no longer has any immune system, zero, nothing with which to fight off infection. Just two short weeks ago he was running around our apartment, laughing, and now he has a tube up his nose, a tube coming out of his chest, and his hair is falling out. He is vomiting, sick and miserable.

And Andrew has just been admitted to the bone marrow unit with respiratory problems and an oxygen saturation in the 70's — more than 25% below normal. This is a big deal, a huge deal! This is not cancer; it's worse. I am shocked by how many people still have not joined the National Marrow Donor Program, or think they are too busy to donate blood.

I leave Matthew's room and come around the corner for Andrew's rounds. Standing next to Justin outside Andrew's room, you can feel the tension. Everyone is on edge; no one saw this coming. I am still not completely clear about what is going on, I just know that Andrew has a nasal cannula in and is receiving oxygen because his oxygen saturation remains low — too low. The doctors begin to discuss the possible causes, and most of them are life-threatening. Everyone is in agreement that we want to proceed with the least invasive tests first. I know the drill. They'll probably start with some X-rays and ultrasounds, an echocardiogram and more blood work and go from there. The next few days go by in a blur. Justin and I continue to switch between Matthew's and Andrew's rooms in the bone marrow unit. We learn that the right side of Andrew's heart is very enlarged, and they have identified several abnormalities on his high-resolution lung CT scan. I try to take notes during rounds, when the doctors review the information they've gotten, so that I can do online searches later to get a bit of a handle on what is happening. It helps me ask our doctor better questions, and it gives me a sense of having at least a little control.

We are no closer to understanding the cause of what's happening to Andrew. Over the last several days he has gotten worse and started needing more oxygen support. But we can't give up — we won't give up — and so we keep going, minute by minute. Justin and I can barely speak, not just because we don't have time as we pass each other in the hall, but because it is taking all the energy we have to keep up with our sons' care, remain focused and stay positive. We are both terrified, and if we stop to think about everything that is happening right now, we will surely collapse and not get back up.

Seeing Andrew leaves me speechless. We have taped baby socks over his hands so he can't pull his nasal cannula out, he is covered in steroid cream to help with his most recent recurrence of skin GVHD, and he has some nasty bruises that won't heal because his immune system just can't keep up, but he smiles and laughs and bounces back and forth the way only he can when he is happy. I am stunned at the resilience of my son and feel like a failure for not being as brave as he is. Then I go into Matthew's room and see my other bald-headed little boy, who has been throwing up for days and lies on his sleeping bag with just his shorts on because of his ongoing fevers and all the leads he has taped to his chest.

What has happened to my precious children? Where did we go wrong? How could so much pain and tragedy fall on one family? I am furious, devastated and terrified. How can this be part of any loving God's plan?

"Things are much more serious than we thought," I say to my parents, trying to stay calm. We are standing in the hall outside Matthew's room in the bone marrow unit. They have come up to Cincinnati to help, since taking care of both boys has been so hectic. I hold back the tears as best I can as I try to explain what has developed over the last twenty-four hours. "Andrew is in the PICU, battling for his life. He has severe pulmonary hypertension, which means he has abnormally high blood pressure in the arteries of his lungs, and this is making the right side of his heart work harder than normal. He 'coded' in the operating room yesterday during his bronchoscopy."

"Coded?" my mom asks, alarmed.

"Yes, he stopped breathing and they had to resuscitate him. He is currently on a ventilator." I can feel the fear radiating off both of my parents, but I keep talking. "When he got into the PICU, Andrew was responding positively to the medicines, and we began to wean his oxygen and ventilator settings. But sometime after midnight that suddenly changed and he has kept going downhill. He had six pulmonary hypertension crises, which means a drop in heart rate, blood pressure and oxygen. Each time the crisis lasted longer and it took more intervention from the doctors to get him stable. They decided to start Andrew on nitric oxide to help open up the arteries in his lungs. Without the intervention of fluids, medicines and more oxygen support he would have died from the lack of blood getting through his heart and to the rest of his body." I take a deep breath and swallow hard, not allowing my tears to break through. My parents are both standing like statues as they listen to me speak. "Several times they had to take him off the ventilator and actually bag him because the ventilator was not giving him enough oxygen." I wipe the tears on the sleeve of my sweatshirt and see that my parents are crying too.

"Andrew is scheduled for a cardiac catheterization and VATS — a video-assisted thoracoscopic surgery on Tuesday morning, if we can get him to that point. They would cut out a few sections of his lungs for pathology and biopsy. However, these are very serious and high-risk tests, and at this point Andrew is not stable enough to go through with it. We don't think he could even withstand going under general anesthesia at this point. So this morning in rounds we discussed the pros and cons of just starting treatment today for his severe pulmonary hypertension instead of waiting for these tests. The medicine is not a cure-all, but it might help relieve some of the hypertension. The reality is, the cause of Andrew's pulmonary hypertension remains unknown and probably always will. The doctors are thinking it is probably caused by either his genetic mutation or an immune complication, since he has had three different donors."

"So what is the plan?" my dad asks.

"Well, we are in the process of getting more X-rays and echocardio-grams, and as soon I get back the doctor is going to put an arterial line in his wrist for better and more accurate blood pressures. Andrew has also developed a high fever, so the potential exists for infection, so they have drawn more labs and we will wait to see if anything grows. But he's already on every anti-everything you can be on." My parents look stunned, and we are all covered in our own tears. I don't give them time to say anything. "I can't stay. I need to get back to Andrew and Justin. Please just stay with Matthew, keep him as comfortable as possible. Don't tell him anything, we will be back down to see him when Andrew is more stable." My parents hug me so tight I can barely breathe and I turn to leave the bone marrow unit and head back to the PICU. My heart is racing, my breathing is labored and my vision is blurred, but I know the way regardless. I have been here before many times.

God, I don't know what the plan is, but I am begging you with all my might, please don't take my sweet Andrew Bear. He has spent his whole life fighting this horrific disease and done it with such grace. He doesn't deserve this nightmare anymore. Please spare him. Please heal his body and you can have mine. Take all the disease from him and give it to me. I know that you can, and I pray that you will.

Chapter 22

Courage doesn't always roar. Sometimes courage is the little voice at the end of the day that says, "I'll try again tomorrow."

— Mary Anne Radmacher

September 5, 2009

*I*knew that night. I knew Andrew was not doing well. I leaned over my sweet baby, who lay with a breathing tube coming out of his mouth. Ever so gently I tried to reposition his lovie to better help support the weight of the tube. It looked like it was pulling on the corner of his mouth and I didn't like that at all. I straightened his blankets and made sure he was completely covered and snuggled in as best I could. Holding his small hand I whispered into his ear the same thing he had heard so many times before in his short life.

"Andrew Bear, it's Mommy. I am here and I love you. I know you are tired, so very tired of fighting for your life every single day, but please give Mommy and Daddy a sign. If you're done, then let us know, but if you want to keep fighting then give us a sign." Soon after that, Andrew had the first of several pulmonary hypertension crises. I knew.

It was a night from hell and in the early morning, when we had again just finished getting Andrew somewhat stable, our PICU doctor and our cardiologist came to speak to us. We briefly discussed last night's events, and then I just asked them, point-blank, "Is Andrew dying?" Standing in my pajamas between two of the smartest doctors in the hospital, I choked on my tears. "I believe in my heart he is, and I don't want to hurt him any-more or put him through any more pain. If there is nothing more to do, then please let us know so we can spare him any more suffering."

Both of the doctors looked at me and without much hesitation said, "No. We don't think he is dying yet. He is a very sick little boy, but we feel that we still have some time. We want to talk to you about some options that we would like to try this afternoon if we can get him stable." Both doctors proceeded to talk about the options, their ideas, how they could help Andrew. We talked about crazy things like taking Andrew into surgery and putting a hole in his heart to relieve the pressure, a short-term fix for a long-term problem. We talked about even more options, but my mind was not completely there because I knew we wouldn't get to that point.

I have seen it done before on TV, but it was never like this. The chest compressions are done with such force that I truly think they are going to break Andrew's ribs. Every few minutes the doctors switch because of the physical toll it is taking on them — they are actually sweating. The PICU attending physician stands at the foot of the bed giving orders like a general in the army; serious, matter-of-fact and not missing a beat. There is no chaos in the room despite the number of people there. Medicines are being given, vitals are being checked, blood gases are being checked: everything is happening precisely as ordered.

I am so very thankful for Dr. Wright, the PICU doctor who has been caring for Andrew. He is serious and very sharp. He is meticulous in his appearance, speech, the overall way he conducts himself, and the care he administers to his patients. I notice more and more nurses and doctors gathering outside our room, I suppose to help if needed, but I'm not sure how many more people we can fit in this room.

Standing there watching so many people work so hard to save my son's life is horrific. I cry and cry and just keep saying, "Please don't hurt my baby." Justin can't watch and stands at the window with his back to the scene, but I can't turn away. I stand next to Andrew, as close as I can be without getting in the way. He isn't crying, but his belly just keeps getting bigger and bigger the more they push on it to try and force air into his tiny body.

After what seems like an eternity I finally cry out, "Please! Enough is enough. Just be done, please don't hurt my baby anymore." Justin grabs me and says, "No, let them keep trying. They'll tell us when it's enough." We stand there holding each other for dear life. I can't stop crying and am beginning to hyperventilate. My eyes go from the doctors doing chest compressions to my baby's tiny body, back to the monitor and back to the chest compressions — it is a scene from a horror movie. Dr. Wright comes over and very calmly says, "Please give us a few more minutes. I understand your wishes, and I will tell you when we have done everything we can, but we are not there yet."

I am not sure how much more time goes by before I hear the most horrific words ever: "I'm sorry Mr. and Mrs. Akin, I think we are done. There is nothing more we can do." The room becomes deathly quiet as everyone waits to hear what to do next. Without thinking I begin to speak.

"Please get all the tubes out of him, turn off all the machines and leave the room." And as fast it had filled up, as fast did it empty. Justin and I hold each other and cry while Andrew lies motionless on his hospital bed. We both shake with pain. I gasp for air and the more I try to breathe the more difficult it becomes. All we can muster from our lips is, "We're sorry, we are so very sorry."

Andrew Preston Akin, my second born child is dead, and he was only two years and three months old. It was two years ago to the day that he was diagnosed with the most hideous words I have ever heard: hemophagocytic lymphohistiocytosis. HLH. The following Labor Day weekend we learned his HLH was back after having his second bone marrow transplant. Now it is Labor Day weekend again and our Andrew Bear is gone.

Not knowing what to do, but going into action without thinking, I begin to do what I have done so many times before. I gather Andrew's bath supplies and begin to fill the little pink bucket. I open the sliding glass door that separates our living nightmare from the rest of the world. I ask our nurse for some clean towels and washcloths and begin to undress my son. I talk to him as if he is still here. I make sure not to get his central line dressing wet, not that it matters now, but somehow it does to me. I bathe him gently, lovingly, as I have done a million times before. I dry him off, despite my tears wetting his little body. I continue in my rhythm as I put on a clean diaper and begin to rub his lavender lotion all over him. I comb his hair and clean out his ears and finally dress him in a clean pair of pajamas. As I pick him up, some blood starts to run out of his nose and mouth, but I don't care; I just gently wipe it away and reassure him that it's OK, Mommy and Daddy are here. I wrap Andrew up in one of his favorite blankets and put one of his lovies in his hand.

I sit down in the rocking chair and begin to rock my son. Justin kneels next to me and we cry and cry and cry. We can't stop telling him how proud we are of him and how much we love him. Our apologies continue. We can't stop saying we're sorry, over and over and over. Despite the final trauma he just endured, he looks so peaceful, almost like he is sleeping. I cannot believe he is dead.

Justin and I sit there in complete and utter shock. My sweet Andrew Bear is gone? Just like that, after all he went through, is that it? I just don't understand! I want to sit here forever, and I barely even want to hand Andrew over to Justin, but I do. We sit and cry together while talking about what an amazingly brave little boy we have. At some point we are interrupted by a knock on the door. It is the chaplain. She has come to talk to us about arrangements.

The only thing worse than holding your dead child is having to think about what to do with his body. We can't go home and think about it or take time to let the shock pass off, because we have another child who is sick and needs us. We won't be leaving this hospital for a while. We look at the list of funeral homes and ask for a recommendation. All we know is that we want Andrew cremated. And if this was not enough horror for one lifetime, we must also decide if Andrew should have an autopsy. It is all unbelievable, and I still have to walk back to the bone marrow unit to tell my parents their grandson has just died. I can barely leave Andrew to go back to the unit.

I open our sliding door in the PICU, take a step outside, and look around. I am changed forever. I walk with my head down; I feel as though I might throw up any second. As I walk through the double doors of the bone marrow unit, I can feel several sets of eyes on me. I know the nurses know what just happened. They can see the monitors in the PICU from the front desk. But no one says anything and I go on to Matthew's room. I knock on the heavy wooden door and stick my head in. I manage to force a smile. I say a brief hello to my Matthew Man and reassure him his daddy and I will be back with him soon. My parents step out of the room and I grab both of their hands. We walk over to the window at the end of the hall, and somehow I choke the words out: "Andrew has died."

They both begin to crumble, but I tell them if they want to see him they need to come now. Amy, our nurse, is nearby and knows what to do without me asking; she is so good that way.

Time seems to stand still as we sit rocking Andrew, and yet there could never be enough time. Finally Justin and I realize we need to say our final good-byes, that we need to get back to Matthew, who is very sick himself.

The nurse comes in our room with a wheelchair so I can sit and hold Andrew. He is all bundled up in my arms and Justin walks next to us as we are escorted to the morgue. We choose to take him because we want to be the last people to hold him. We don't want him to feel like we left him, not for a minute. We ride down in a private elevator with a cop — not sure why we need the police escort because I don't think anyone wants to join us. The elevator doors open and we head down a short hallway. I can see the open door of the morgue ahead. I stand and take notice of my surroundings. It looks a lot like they do on TV: a basic room with a scale hanging from the ceiling, metal tables and the metal drawers on the wall where they keep the bodies. The more I look, the louder my sobs become. Justin and I kiss and hug Andrew until we just can't stand to be there anymore and then I gently lay him down on the metal table. I keep trying to tell myself he is no longer in there, that he has left that broken body, that it is OK, but I am literally about to pass out. Leaving Andrew behind is the most difficult thing I have ever done.

And then we turn back towards the elevator, ride it up to the PICU, walk back into the room where Andrew just died and begin to pack up our things. In the last two days, we have lost three kids from our bone marrow unit. Just the day before, a teenage boy, Troy, passed away and earlier this morning a young college woman, Kari, died, and now Andrew. Our small bone marrow community has been rocked. On the short walk back to the unit, we agree not to tell Matthew. He is scared and fighting his own battle and he doesn't need any more to deal with. Wiping away the tears the best we can, we walk into our only living son's room and try to surround him with our love and support. We send my parents home. As much as they want to stay and help, Justin and I need to do this together. I'm sure we are still in shock; how could we not be? But Matthew needs us and so we do what we have done for the past two years: dig deeper and keep going.

Chapter 23

You will not find the answers you seek amongst the noise of the world,
the answers lie within the silence of time.

—Unknown

September 2009

*L*ying in my sleeping bag next to Matthew, I listen to him and
Justin breathe. I am awake and have been for quite a while.
The anxiety of what lies ahead has kept me from sleeping. I keep my tears
quiet — I have become a master at that — while I watch the numbers on
the monitor change as Matthew breathes. I see that one of his IV medicine
pumps is almost done and will soon beep, so I get up, silence it and then
call for the nurse. Once she comes in I know the boys will wake up.

Things are tight in our room. Matthew and I are sleeping together,
Justin is on the pull-out chair/bed, and only our most basic belongings can
be squeezed in. I don't care that our room is small, and I don't care that I
have been sleeping in a sleeping bag and eating in a hospital cafeteria for
months. All I care about is getting Matthew better and moving our life forward, away from all this tragedy and heartbreak. And today, all I care
about is making it through every parent's worst nightmare somehow, some
way. I am praying that I will find strength I never knew I had, because I
know I'll need it.

Ever since we walked back into the bone marrow unit after Andrew
died, the staff has been amazing. Amy, our primary nurse, has made sure
that the normal daily traffic of hospital personnel stays out of our room.
At this point, I don't want anybody stopping by. From the chaplain to
child life, I will reach out to them if we want them. No one really knows
what to say because it is more than Andrew dying: it is being stuck in the
hospital still with another sick child. It is the fact that no one knows when
we will get discharged, let alone allowed to go back home to St. Louis. We
can't plan a memorial, and we both continue to try and hide our heartbreak from Matthew. There are no words for what we're going through,
and we know that.

Justin and I take turns showering and getting ready. The bathroom in Matthew's room is small, but believe me, I am not complaining. Normally parents can't even use their child's bathroom, so this is a luxury. Not having to use the parents' lounge bathroom is a gift; the staff is trying to give us as much privacy as possible.

As I begin to comb out my wet hair Matthew asks inquisitively, "Mommy, why are you and Daddy getting so dressed up? Where are you going?"

I respond quickly, "Matthew Man, Mommy and Daddy have an important meeting with some doctors today, so we will have to leave for a little while. But Nurse Amy and Sam from physical therapy will be here with you. I am sure you guys will have fun while we are gone." That entire sentence was just one big, fat lie. We are not meeting with any doctors, and I would hardly consider lying in bed in the bone marrow unit, hanging out with a nurse and physical therapist to be fun, even though they are both great women. I try to finish getting ready, but I cannot keep my eyes dry long enough to put my makeup on.

The decisions that have to be made immediately upon someone's death are intense, and although they're the last things you want to think about, they are necessary. Justin and I decided that a partial autopsy should be done on Andrew's heart and lungs. We had to know what went wrong. What caused this sudden condition? Could we have done anything differently to save him? Everyone thought Andrew was on his way to being a long-term survivor when, out of the blue, he became very sick with pulmonary complications he had never experienced before, and within a week he was gone. Besides, after everything he went through during his lifetime we felt it was imperative to learn something and not let his death be in vain. We were also afraid that the genetic mutation might have been a possible cause and wanted to know if there was anything we could learn that might protect Matthew. But all that being said, the thought of an autopsy on your baby is life-changing. I tell myself all the reasons over and over and they make sense to the logical side of my brain, but when the emotional side steps in, the thought of the autopsy leaves a part of me dead inside. It is a wound I will live with forever, and that's OK.

Thankfully, we do not have far to go, but nothing could have prepared me for the sight in front of my eyes. The building is small, old and not very well-maintained. There are only one or two cars in the parking lot, and as we pull around I see what looks like a chimney and realize what it is for. My heart is beating so hard I can barely breathe. Justin sees that I am struggling more and more to get a deep breath. He takes my hand and squeezes it and we begin to cry together, out loud, as we wait for our son to arrive.

Within minutes we see Lee, the funeral director. I chose him from a long list of funeral homes because he just happened to be at the top of the list, but we found that he could not be a kinder or more compassionate man. We had a left a message the morning Andrew died, and almost immediately he called us back, willing to meet us early to pick out an urn. He is exactly what I needed and he has gladly accommodated every detailed request between picking Andrew up from the morgue at Children's to now. Lee answered all my questions and took care of Andrew just as I requested, keeping me in the loop every step of the way. Lee and I discussed everything and he made sure my wishes were followed. As we talked, I kept thinking, *what a horrific job*, but at the same time I wanted to hug Lee nonstop for helping me through this darkest hour. If it was possible to provide any peace at that moment, Lee did, and that is indescribably valuable. Lee is a gift to us and Andrew at a time when I didn't think that was possible.

Justin and I get out of the car and head into this small building that houses nothing more than countless urns holding the ashes of dead people. The only sound is our own shoes on the concrete floor as we make our way into the poorly decorated chapel where we will sit as our son is being cremated.

It was not a point of discussion; we both knew this was where we belonged. We never left him in life, and we will not leave him in death. With Andrew getting sick at such a young age, he always seemed to stay our baby, which in many ways was a gift in itself. His growth was stunted from all the steroids and he was inpatient for so long that he got behind on his developmental milestones. But we both believed that when Andrew got through all of this he would catch up. I always cherished sleeping with Andrew, snuggling him, holding him. I realize that I was able to hold him more than many mothers hold their children in a lifetime. How could we ever bury him in the ground and leave him somewhere? At least this way we could bring him home with us. He will always be with us, no matter where we live.

Justin and I sit alone in the front pew, waiting. The chapel is old, with cinder block walls that look cold and industrial. There is purple decoration, which doesn't look like a single church I have ever been in. I don't like it at all. I had decided it was not a good idea for me to see Andrew at this point, but I wanted Lee to make sure of several things. He enters now and lets us know that things are about to get started if we are ready. We simply nod. And then, when I thought things could not get worse, I am shaken to my core with the loudest, most awful sound that can fill my ears: the sound of my baby being cremated.

Chapter 24

Think of your child; then, not as dead, but as living; not as a flower that has withered, but as one that is transplanted, and touched by a divine hand, is blooming in richer colors and sweeter shades than those of earth.

—Richard Hooker

September 2009

My entire world has been turned upside down and nothing seems right anymore. In the days since Andrew's death and cremation, I can't stop thinking about what I can do to honor him. I feel almost compulsive about it. Whatever I do, it can't just be about his death. Justin is in complete agreement that we don't want people focusing on that; Andrew was so much more.

Now it seems the perfect thing has come along. We have decided to go to Yosemite National Park to do the Histio Hike For A Cure in three weeks. September is national Histiocytosis Awareness Month so it almost seems like a sign. The hike is going to be grueling, physically and emotionally. It is an 18-mile round trip to Half Dome, 10–14 hours. I am in no shape physically to be doing this hike, but I am more than ready mentally. Especially because we don't know when we will be back in St. Louis to have Andrew's service, we are both longing to do something now, and this seems like a great opportunity. Ideally, I would love this to become an annual trip for our family. I like the thought of going out there in years to come with Matthew and hiking together as a family to honor our son and his brother. The only problem is we have told Matthew about the hike and he keeps begging to go. The fight and spirit of my little boy leaves me speechless. He wants to go so badly, but all we can do is promise that next year we will all go.

Every time we say that I hope that God hears and answers our prayers. I have never been to Yosemite but I've seen the pictures and I can hardly wait. I think it will be so therapeutic to be outside in nature, soaking up all the natural beauty God has to offer. Until then we just keep going one day at a time. Matthew seems to be doing fairly well and I pray that this will continue.

Today is the big day and I can't stop thinking about Justin. Not surprisingly, I am not in Yosemite and Justin is. That's OK. Our plans and Matthew's health are not on the same page, and in the weeks leading up to the hike he got so sick that I can't leave him. Justin and I talked about it at length and I shed some tears of disappointment, but we agreed that it was best for me to stay with Matthew while Justin went to Yosemite. Justin has been joined by his friend Jeff so he doesn't have to hike alone, and that makes me feel better. I am sad that I can't go, but I know my place is here with Matthew. Yosemite isn't going anywhere; I'll get there soon enough.

I hope the weather is good, that they're safe, don't get hurt, and most importantly that Justin gets the healing he is looking for. I run down to the cafeteria right at 11:30, when they first start serving lunch. My friend Lisa and I like to be there before anyone else, hopefully avoiding extra germs. Standing in line at the salad bar I make the same plate of vegetables I have made a hundred times before. I can't stop thinking about Andrew and Justin hiking today. Somehow as I turn the corner to get my soda, I trip and drop my tray. As my salad goes flying all over the cafeteria floor, it is the proverbial straw that broke the camel's back. Overcome with emotion, I sit on the floor, sobbing and trying to scoop up my mess.

A cafeteria worker runs to my aid. She kneels down and insists that everything will be OK, that I can get another salad, that she won't even charge me, as I continue to sob. Finally, I am able to calm down enough to explain, "It's not about the salad." I burst into more tears as I continue to clean up my mess. I explain that my baby just died a few weeks ago and my only other son is fighting for his life too. The cafeteria worker is speechless as she continues to help me. I can feel people staring at me and why wouldn't they? I finally manage to get myself back together and leave the cafeteria empty-handed. Food no longer sounds good.

Later that night Justin posts an update on our CarePage.

Well, we did it! My friend Jeff and I, with a little help from Andrew, hiked over 18 miles to the top of Half Dome in Yosemite. We left at 5:30 in the morning and got back at 5:30 in the evening. The total elevation gain on the hike was a mile. Thank you to everyone who supported Team Andrew Akin. The hike was spectacular, awe-inspiring, beautiful, strenuous and dangerous. Now I can see why over 60 people have perished doing this hike and why the National Park Service has considered closing the top of Half Dome. I shot a lot of video, which I'll edit and post on the next update.

Jeff and I hiked further than everyone else because we missed one of the turns and headed in the wrong direction. All day long we had passed hikers and we usually said a quick "hi" or "good morning" to each other. About a half-mile after we missed our turn, by the grace of God we came across a couple that had stopped to eat a snack. Instead of saying "hi" like everyone else, they asked us where we were going. When we answered "Half Dome," they told us that we were going the wrong way and that we had missed the turn. If that couple hadn't been at that exact point at that exact time we could have hiked for miles and miles until we realized our mistake. Thank you, Andrew Bear!

To get to the top of Half Dome you have to go up the "cables." When I saw the "cables" my first thought was, "Are you kidding me? The National Parks Service actually lets the general public do this? This is crazy!" The incline is so steep that you have to pull yourself up using the cables and every ten yards or so there is a board that you can put your feet on. Otherwise, you'll just slide down the mountain into oblivion. The total distance of the cables is around 425 feet. It felt like 425 yards!

As Jeff and I were putting on our gloves getting ready for our climb up the cables, a cell phone and water bottle came tumbling down the mountain from someone who was obviously having some issues halfway up. We were glad that a cell phone and water bottle were the only things that came down. As they disappeared down the mountain we were reminded of the danger ahead. Our biggest fear was not that one of us would make a mistake but that someone else would and take us with them. But we made it to the top and then had lunch with a pretty amazing view. Once again, thank you to everyone who supported Team Andrew Akin. So far, we've raised $19,166 for the Histiocytosis Association of America. We raised more money than any other team. Thank you! In total, this year's hike has raised $175,000. Over 250 people from across the country came to Yosemite for this year's Hike For A Cure and it was very nice to meet some fellow Histio families who follow our journey on CarePages. After the Saturday night dinner I was asked to introduce Dr. Edwards to the group before she gave her speech. It was an honor!

I would hardly consider myself a runner per se and if you know me with my short legs, standing five feet tall, you'll know I don't have the typical runner's body. But before the boys came along I decided to train and run my first half-marathon with Team in Training. When I saw the flyer that came in the mail something about it called to me, and I went to the informational meeting at our local library. After that I was all in-training, raising money, everything. I loved the feeling of crossing that finish line: me, running a half-marathon! It felt good. I ran another race a few years later and even ran one soon after Andrew was diagnosed for Team Andrew to raise money and awareness for HLH.

It has now been a good two years that I have been living in the hospital with almost no exercise, but something has come along that I can't pass up. I believe this is my "hike." I have decided to run the inaugural Rick Hendrick Half Marathon in Concord, North Carolina in six weeks! Rick Hendrick, chairman and CEO of Hendrick Motorsports, established the Hendrick Marrow Program in 1997 after he was diagnosed with leukemia. Even though he didn't need a marrow transplant himself, he wanted to help other patients who were waiting to find a marrow match and a second chance at life. Running this race will be my tribute to Andrew this year since I couldn't go to Yosemite with Justin. I am excited about the opportunity to do something myself to honor Andrew and support a very important organization that has helped provide life to my boys. Saving the world isn't easy, but saving a life is.

Realistically, I am not physically ready to run this half-marathon, but mentally I'm in. The past several weeks have been tough. We have been in and out of the hospital and so my training suffered, but I had known it would. Justin and Matthew drop me off at the airport and before long it's time to board for Charlotte. It is hard for me to take it all in: I am getting ready to go run a half-marathon in memory of my one son and in honor of my other son. Sitting on the plane I look around at everyone, wondering why they are going to Charlotte. When we arrive, I am a bundle of nerves — not sure which emotion is about to come over me at any minute. My only goal is to show up, run until I can't run anymore, and then walk if I have to until I finish. I double-check my alarm, make sure all my running gear is laid out, and then I lie in bed for what seems like hours trying to fall asleep.

Up before my alarm, I start eating a PowerBar and laugh while I do, because I know that it is going to take a lot more than a PowerBar to get me through 13.1 miles today. Proudly wearing my specially designed T-shirt with pictures of both boys, I make my way to the start of the race. It is cool this morning, almost cold, but actually perfect weather for running. I am not sure how many people to expect since this is the first year for this race. The course is unique as we will be running in and around the Lowe's Motor Speedway, not the usual city streets. I pin my number to the front of my shirt, not wanting to cover up the boys' faces. Ironically I am number one. Talking to fellow runners and members of Hendrick Motor Sports this morning is the perfect distraction, but before long it is time to start. I guess there are no more than fifty people in the race, and soon we are off running together in a small pack. *God, please stay with me. Help me finish this race for Andrew and Matthew. Let them be proud of their mommy.*

There are few spectators along the course, which is fine, because I am lost in thought about why I am here. I talk to Andrew and then I try my best to think of all the kids that have passed away from St. Louis Children's and Cincinnati Children's — I want them to know that their lives were not in vain. Many times I call on Andrew to help me, to keep me going, to lighten my load, as this is a very hard race for me, not being in good shape. But quit? Never!

I am making it, slow and steady, until I hit mile 11, when, as they say in the runners' world, I hit the wall. But out of nowhere, the race director pulls up next to me on a bike.

"You are the last runner out," he said, "but I have heard your story and you are one tough lady. I am going to stay with you for the rest of the race." I am so grateful because at this point I become physically overwhelmed with grief. I can hardly breathe as the tears flow nonstop. I slow down a bit to try and catch my breath, but my emotions get the best of me. The reality of what has happened, that I will never get my son back, that we are still fighting to save Matthew is more than I can contain. Slowly but surely I make my way to the very end of the course. I round the last corner and look up to see all the runners and volunteers surrounding the finish line yelling my name — cheering me on as if I were their best friend. My already streaming tears go up to nothing short of hysteria. I am absolutely flabbergasted: all these people stayed around to cheer me on. The Hendrick Team had let everyone know that I was about to finish. I am moved beyond words and humbled to my knees. I can barely stand the love and affection that is being poured on me. It is the perfect ending to a perfect race. I will be forever grateful to each and every one of those people who helped me finish strong for my boys. There are lots of hugs and pictures and tears. It is perfect. I am tired but so fulfilled. I have finished what I came to do.

When I leave the hotel the sky is gray and rain has begun to fall. A huge smile crosses my face. *Thank you Andrew and all the angels for smiling down on us this morning with the beautiful sun.* Within a few hours I am safely back in Cincinnati with my boys. I am so very thankful that I had the opportunity to go and do this for my boys. Justin and I will be eternally grateful for being able to get away. While we had to go separately, it worked out perfectly. We needed this time to honor our son. Andrew might be physically gone from this world but in actuality he will live on, perhaps more than he did in life.

Chapter 25

Strength does not come from physical capacity. It comes from an indomitable will.
—Mahatma Gandhi

September 2009

My eyes dart from the monitor, reading each number as if it were a message from God, back to the doctor, trying to see some sign of hope, some sign that maybe, just maybe, he is stable. But somehow I know. My mommy instinct tells me, much as I don't want to accept it, that Matthew is going downhill — and fast. His nonstop vomiting and diarrhea have taken away eight pounds of my son in three days. My firstborn son, my adventurer, my little boy who knows no fear now lies in a hospital bed, pale, lifeless and bald. He has no strength to do anything, and he couldn't if he wanted to with so many lines connecting him to machines and monitors.

Just four short weeks ago we checked into the bone marrow unit together, ready to take this genetic mutation head-on. Justin and Andrew were living in our temporary apartment, and we all believed we were on our way out of hell. Upon checking into the bone marrow unit, Matthew quickly shared his smile, his laughter and his adventure for life with every person who came into our room. I could not have been more proud of him. I almost laugh when I think I had to remind him that he couldn't jump on the bed while playing Wii sports during his first days of chemo, but I don't, because when I look at him now it seems impossible that that ever really happened. What wouldn't I do to see him jump on the bed again.

Despite their best efforts, Matthew is not responding to the myriad of interventions. The nurse continues to fill a gigantic plastic syringe with fluid and push it straight into Matthew's central line, hoping it will raise his dangerously low blood pressure. Again, the doctor orders more fluid and more medicine, and we all look at the monitors for a sign of improvement. Still nothing. The tension mounts as Matthew's pressure drops still further, and I can hardly stand another minute when I realize this is not going to be enough. I catch Dr. Chase's eyes, and they tell me what I already know: we are out of time.

Things begin to move even faster. One nurse unplugs everything that is hooked to the wall, while another nurse unlocks the wheels on Matthew's bed. I grab a clean blanket and loosely drape it over Matthew's face and head to protect him from infection as we wheel him out of our safe zone and into the germ-filled halls. Justin holds our door open and helps the nurses maneuver the bed as I wrap myself around Matthew and hold on to him for dear life.

I quietly whisper in his ear, "It's going to be OK, Buddy, Mommy and Daddy are here." I just repeat it over and over as we are pushed with as much force and speed as possible out of the bone marrow unit. Everyone in the hallway sees us coming, and a few stop to hold open the double doors that separate the bone marrow unit from the rest of the hospital. We roll through the doorway, turn the corner and head to the PICU. We pass by a few familiar people — other doctors and therapists from our unit and their faces immediately say, "Oh, no." I just hold Matthew tighter and swallow hard to choke back my tears. The PICU is not physically far from the bone marrow unit, but at a time like this, it feels as if it's miles away. Two weeks ago Andrew passed away in the PICU and now we're passing through the last set of double doors to come in again with Matthew.

A nurse is ahead of us holding the doors. There is a small hallway that separates the PICU from everything else; it has a slight incline and so our nurses begin to gather speed because getting the hospital bed over it takes some force. As we enter the small hallway, my first thought is of heaven: it reminds me of heaven. Not that I have been there or had anyone report back to me on what it's like, but this is what I picture. It is bright and white. Perhaps it's the frosted glass on either side glowing with light from outside. How ironic that this place would make me think of heaven.

They push us past the room Andrew died in two weeks earlier. I can't even begin to process that because all of my fear is wrapped up in Matthew right now. I see an empty room just ahead with the double doors already open. They swing the bed around and up against the freshly painted wall, and I jump off to make room for all the nurses and doctors who need to be in my space. Immediately the doctor starts to give orders, and the nurses move quickly to draw up medicines and connect Matthew to the monitors in the room as the orders keep coming. Justin and I are holding on to each other for dear life, crying, and watching our only living son fight for his life. The monitor shows Matthew's first blood pressure since we arrived: 47/20.

"Please, Dr. Chase, you can't let Matthew die!"

Chapter 26

The purpose of prayer is not to influence God to grant you special favors, but rather to remind yourself that you are always connected to God.
—Dr. Wayne W. Dyer

September 2009

*T*oday is day +17. It has been seventeen days since Matthew received his bone marrow transplant and seven days since my sweet Andrew Bear left this earth. I remain overwhelmed at the enormity of our situation, but if there is any light at the end of this tunnel, there is a small glimmer today: we are getting discharged from the hospital. Even though we know we are far from leaving Cincinnati, we are thankful to be heading to our apartment. It will be hard to go there for many reasons. We have downsized from a two bedroom apartment to a one-bedroom because we now without part of our family. The physical task of moving could not have come at a more inopportune time. But a few friends came to help and made it easy, and perhaps the was a gift in disguise in some strange way, because the distraction of our friends was exactly what we needed.

But going home to the apartment also means we will finally have to tell Matthew what happened to his baby brother. No matter how much I read on "how to tell a sibling," it doesn't seem to help.

Within minutes of being home Matthew's personality has started to emerge. I would not believe it I weren't seeing it for myself. He is literally coming back to life and nothing could lift our spirits more right now. Matthew is still very weak and can hardly walk, but I am optimistic that with some time away from the hospital we will be able to get him moving again. Our talk with Matthew about Andrew went smoothly. I don't know why I am surprised; he never ceases to amaze me, every day. He never asked about Andrew again for the rest of the time in the hospital after he died. Somehow, I think he knew despite our best efforts to keep it from him.

Being dead and never coming back is a hard concept for a kid of almost five years old to grasp. Kids that age barely understand the concept of time, and their place in it, so "forever" is a tricky word. And the urn is not easy to explain either. However, it is good to have something to show Matthew, and for him to touch. In typical Matthew fashion, he is handling this way better than we are, and I am in awe of my son. But being in the apartment without Andrew is like missing a limb: you can still function, but not nearly as well, and not a minute goes by that you don't think about what is missing and feel the pain of what you used to have. Justin and I remain thankful we decided to have Andrew cremated. Having his urn with us has been so comforting. I can't imagine not having it.

Hopefully, we will only have to spend a few more months in Cincinnati before Matthew will be strong enough to get discharged back home to St. Louis. Then we can finally begin to figure out how to move on with our lives, getting Matthew completely healthy and honoring Andrew.

Less than twenty-four hours after discharge we are already back in the hospital. We literally just got home, had our medical supplies delivered and started to unpack. Justin and I are standing hand in hand at the head of Matthew's bed trying to understand; he was thrilled to be out of the hospital and back in the apartment but within the first few hours of being home he started to complain of stomach pain and began to have uncontrollable diarrhea. I was so frustrated. Not with Matthew; I was so angry that my sweet son can't seem to get a break. I can't stop thinking, *are you kidding me? Has he not gone through enough? We have only been home for hours and he is already in pain again? Please, God, let him feel better, let him get better, please!* And within hours we went from the clinic, to the bone marrow unit, to the PICU. I have seen it before, but it still scares the life out of me how fast kids can go from fine to critical condition. And now we are again living that nightmare as our only living son fights for his life in the PICU.

Is there anything that I could begin to say that would adequately scrape the surface of the pain, the fear and the unfairness of it all? The only thing that has calmed us down is the fact that Matthew has finally stabilized and is resting comfortably. Things are quiet for the moment and that is about as good as we can expect for now. Evening has passed and we are approaching the wee hours of the night, so Justin pulls out the chair/bed and lies down, while I pull up a chair next to Matthew's bed and lay my head on a pillow by his feet. I want to be as close to him as possible, to hold his hand, to hear his breathing without disturbing him.

The doctors think the reason Matthew got so sick was extreme dehy-dration combined with an infection in his bloodstream, making him go septic. However, we will know more in a day or two, as we see whether anything grows from his cultures. I am so tired of infections, sepsis and waiting to see if something grows in the blood cultures. I am tired of watching my children suffer and be sick and fight to live. I am tired of feeling so helpless, sad and angry all at the same time! Please just let him rest peacefully and maybe tomorrow he will be stable enough to go back to the bone marrow transplant unit.

The days start to add up again and I don't see us getting out any time soon. We were wrong about what caused Matthew's PICU stay: it was not a bug, which would have been relatively easy to treat with antibiotics. That would be too easy. Instead, Matthew has been diagnosed with severe graft-versus-host disease of the gut. We have increased his steroids and added a new immune suppression drug to try and help quiet the GVHD. He is depressed and lonely. I am trying so hard to keep his spirits up, but he is no dummy. He knows what he's missing in here, and he hates it. His pain has been hard to manage, and so we have started him on a morphine drip. You have no idea what it is like to hear your child cry out in pain, begging me to "Press the button, Mommy." But I already have, and he can't get any more pain medicine for several minutes. I keep disposable hot packs on his tummy, but it's not enough. We watch Scooby-Doo over and over as a dis-traction, but it is hardly working.

He just keeps asking us when he can go home. And what can I say but, "Not yet, Buddy." There is nothing I want more than for him to get better, get out of here and go home, but there is not a damn thing I can do about it. *I hate my life!* If there was any way I could take this sickness into my body I would have done it years ago, but I remain healthy while my one son is dead and my other one is sick and in pain.

Standing in the shower I cry and cry. I always try to keep it together and put on a brave face for Matthew, for the hospital staff, for my parents, but the shower and the car are my safe zones — my cry zones. I miss Andrew more than words can say; I will never forgive myself for transplanting Matthew; and I just don't want to live anymore. *God, please help me!*

After another long stay in the hospital, twenty-four days to be exact, we are getting discharged again back to the apartment. Thankfully, after this latest nightmare we will be out of the hospital for Matthew's fifth birthday and Halloween, which are only a few days apart. It doesn't seem like much, but we are happy to have anything that might brighten his mood. I continue to try everything I know and can think of to cheer him up. Justin and I have offered to have any type of party, but how much fun is a birthday when you don't feel good, you're stuck in a random apartment away from home, and you have no friends to play with? Birthdays have always been a big deal in our family, so we have tried our best to talk up his birthday, but Matthew is so depressed nothing really matters.

All he wants is to go home and see Charlie, his best friend. I wish more than anything in the world we could give him that. But since that is not an option I am doing the next best thing, which is a far second. We are having a Scooby-Doo party. I bought every single thing they had at the party store with Scooby on it to decorate the apartment. I asked Matthew what kind of birthday cake he wanted, and he said a pumpkin, so I went to Michaels to buy the necessary supplies to make my son the best pumpkin birthday cake ever. Justin and I bought just about every toy he didn't already have, hoping it would put even a small smile on his face, but despite our best efforts we can see that he is miserable and I don't blame him a bit. We are miserable: Andrew just died, Matthew has been sicker than anyone thought and has so many serious complications, and there is no end in sight. I suppose we all try to act excited, not wanting to let each other down.

In the three months after Andrew died, Matthew encountered just as many life-threatening complications as his brother did, only different. He had graft-versus-host disease of the gut so severe the doctors had to keep raising his steroid dosages and adding additional immune suppression drugs to help. Matthew quickly became so bloated none of his clothes fit, and he was moody and hungry all the time. He now looked like one of them: like a sick BMT kid fighting for his life, not the healthy, dark-brown-haired, crystal-blue-eyed little boy who had walked in just six short weeks before. We were devastated. How could this happen? Then, on top of his GVHD he got a virus that caused severe inflammation of the bladder. He began to urinate blood and before long he was passing clots out of his penis. They became larger and more painful until he had to have emergency surgery to remove one of the clots since it was blocking his ability to urinate.

Matthew was definitely not used to taking oral medicines like Andrew and that became a challenge as well. I tried bargaining and begging but nothing worked. So we gave him the option of taking his medicine orally or having an NJ tube placed but he said he preferred that. He is brave beyond his years, but that's not what I want for my son. The NJ tube got placed and he didn't seem to mind, but often he would vomit so much the tube would come up and we would have to place another one, which meant feeding a plastic tube up his nose and down the back of his throat into his stomach. And if he did not have enough going on, because of his rapid weight gain from the steroids and being bedridden, he developed a cardial and pleural effusion. These were all new issues that we did not know anything about, and with every complication we worried more and more. Matthew started his transplant healthy, with no active disease, he was young, and he had a perfect match. On paper, everything lined up to make this look like a smooth process, but hindsight is 20/20.

Somehow, after months of complications, inpatient stays and severe GVHD, we are getting discharged, and not just from the hospital back to our apartment, but from the hospital all the way home to St. Louis. We are leaving Cincinnati after being here for the last eleven months, and we are finally taking our sons home with us. We will be home for Christmas and can begin to plan our memorial service for Andrew.

A big part of why we get to go home is that there is a new doctor in St. Louis. Dr. Narayan did her fellowship at Cincinnati in the BMT unit and will be in constant communication with our team here. Besides, everyone knows how badly we need to be at home as a family, to begin to heal. Matthew is far from out of the woods but has been making strides in the right direction and I know Dr. Edwards would not send us home if she didn't think it was safe. There are so many things to look forward to at home, like the brand-new playroom that my parents built for Matthew while we have been in Cincinnati, and the new bunk beds that we promised him once he started the transplant process. We kept telling Matthew that once he got better, his best friend Charlie could come sleep over. Finally, I am optimistic, for the first time in a long time, that he is on the road to recovery.

Lying on our couch, snuggled up under a big, soft blanket, I look at the simple white lights on our artificial Christmas tree. It is a reminder of how much our lives have changed since Andrew first got sick. We use to have real trees, but not anymore: they pose a serious risk for bone marrow transplant patients because of the bacteria they carry. But I couldn't care less about the tree; we put it up for Matthew. All the decorations we put up are for him, to try to make things feel normal, happy, good. The only sound I hear at this hour is our furnace blowing warm air into our home. Justin is sleeping with Matthew tonight. We have been taking turns sleeping with him since he can't walk and needs help going to the bathroom, and he is connected to different pumps that run throughout the night.

I am a boiling pot about to bubble over any minute. I am consumed with grief and despair, but at the same time overwhelmed with gratitude. Thinking about Andrew's death leaves me gasping for air and apologizing to him, but while I squeeze his bear lovie I begin to laugh at a memory. This silly lovie almost caused me a heart attack.

Back in the fall after Andrew had died, and while Matthew was inpatient, my lovie disappeared. I frantically tore apart our room trying to find that lovie. I had been sleeping with it every night since Andrew died, and it is extremely important to me. After I turned our room upside down and there was no sign of it. I thought it must have gotten wrapped up in the fitted sheet and went to the linen room in the hospital. I begged to go down and search for it, but they wouldn't let me. They sent one of our nurse assistants down, but she came back empty-handed. In desperation we called the company that picks up and washes the hospital linens. If they found a 12 × 12 light-brown square with a bear's head and "Andrew" embroidered on it in brown they were to please call us.

Several days went by and I was resigned that my Andrew Bear lovie was gone for good. And then, like the one unexpected gift you didn't see under the tree, I heard a knock on our door and there stood two women from the linen company holding a small ziplock bag with my Andrew Bear lovie in it. I began to cry and hugged them. Everyone was shocked that it was found, but I now know that it was a gift to ease my grief. And now, lying on my couch, I cannot find words big enough to describe my gratitude for being home in our house for Christmas, with Matthew. Everybody thought Matthew would do so well; nothing could have prepared us for all of these serious and rare complications. We thought we had seen it all with Andrew. He had every rare and odd complication and after three bone marrow transplants, what could be left?

My eyes are heavy and wet with tears as I pull the blanket up closer around me. *God, help me please. I am so sad, so scared, so worn out I don't even know what to ask for anymore. I just don't know what to do. Please, I am begging yet again, please just let Matthew get better and let us move past this nightmare.* My eyes close, and I fall asleep.

Chapter 27

Anytime you suffer a setback or disappointment,
put your head down and plow ahead.
—Les Brown

Christmas 2009

*B*eing at home is the best medicine possible; we see Matthew's personality continue to emerge and his depression lessen a little more with each day. When we first got home, he was unable to walk and had not walked in months. The doctors told us that for every day spent lying in a hospital bed, you should allow a week to rebuild that strength. However, when he saw his new playroom that was all it took to get him started.

The playroom is awesome — a kid's dreamland. Toys fill the room, books fill the shelves, there is a big TV to play Wii and the coolest twenty-five-foot-long train table built in against the back wall. This was my dad's idea and it is fantastic. We even have a craft corner with a table and a cabinet full of art supplies. Justin did an amazing job setting everything up, from building the most elaborate train tracks on his new train board to writing, "Welcome home, Matthew" on the chalk board wall. Everything is perfect; not a detail is overlooked. Nothing could have been better than to see him crawl around the room, pulling his backpack full of the pumps he is connected to behind him. Within a few days, Matthew is scooting up and down the steps and could not be loving his playroom more. For the first time in a long time, it feels like we are on our way out of HLH hell. Maybe, just maybe, we can start a new chapter, one without bone marrow transplants, sickness and death.

Tonight is my night to sleep with Matthew. When I am finally finished with everything downstairs, I start to slowly climb in over him, since he went to bed hours ago, but I feel wetness and my heart drops. I know Matthew didn't wet the bed, so I grab my cell phone and use the light from that, not wanting to wake him. I immediately see what has happened and go get Justin. One of the clamps on Matthew's central line had not been unclamped and the pressure in the line had built up until it burst. The moisture I felt was from the medicine that was running out into Matthew's bed and not into his body. Not only is he not getting the medicine he needs, his central line is broken and is open to the outside, putting him at a huge risk of infection.

Luckily, with my two and half years' experience with central lines, I know what to do. Justin gets the supplies as I list them off, and I begin by scrubbing my hands and putting on sterile gloves. I have to assess the risk for Matthew. Is it better to repair the line for the night and keep him home until we can have an appointment first thing in the morning? This keeps him out of the ER, which is the dirtiest place in the hospital, and the residents working the night shift will almost certainly have no experience with repairing a central line anyway. I call our doctor and she agrees that my makeshift sterile patch is good for the night and we will fix it in the morning. Justin feels awful about it, but as I secure Matthew's line, I reassure him that accidents happen. We have been doing our best for two and half years, yet I know we both feel that it's never enough.

It turns out to be a good thing we didn't take Matthew to the ER during the night, since our new hospital, Cardinal Glennon, doesn't carry the repair kit for the kind of line Matthew has. They send a nurse to St. Louis Children's Hospital to get one. In addition, we start Matthew on an additional antibiotic, just to be safe, since he did have an open line that could have picked up an infection, even though he is already on antivirals, antifungals and antibacterials. I'm thankful that they're able to repair the line without having to pull it and surgically insert a new one.

Matthew is enjoying being home and so are we. It's especially tough being without our Andrew Bear in the holiday season, but it gives us all the more reason to give Matthew the best Christmas ever! The days fly by, since we still spend most of them in the clinic. Matthew still needs blood and platelet transfusions and has several drugs that he must get in-clinic because they can't be given at home. But I don't mind; I am happy to spend a few days a week in-clinic so we can stay outpatient. Matthew is so good. He has not complained once since this whole bone marrow transplant process started. God knows he has endured more than a lifetime's worth of pain but he does not yell or cry or scream. He is brave and stoic and could teach most adults I know — including me — many lessons.

It is Christmas morning and I could not be filled with more conflicting feelings. My gratitude runs over for being home and seeing Matthew make such progress over the last few weeks, but my heart is broken for his continued struggles and the loss of Andrew. We try to be excited, filling the family room with every toy we think Matthew would remotely like. We read the letter Santa left him and take note of how much soup Rudolph drank. I loved Matthew's idea this year of leaving him hot soup since he would be so cold. In spite of going through the motions, our true emotions are lacking. Matthew is sweet, and so appreciative of his toys, but we can tell that all he really wants is the one thing we cannot give him: his old self back. And all we want is to make him better. I try so desperately to hide my tears for Matthew's sake, but then I feel like I am cheating Andrew. *Will someone please tell me the right thing to do, to feel, to say?*

They say fact is stranger than fiction and I believe it. You couldn't make this stuff up. I had just finished lighting the candles, setting out the appetizers and making sure everything is just so when my mother-in-law and Justin's grandfather arrive from Texas. Within twenty minutes of them being here, I run downstairs to grab something and am greeted by two inches of sewer water in the basement. I stand there for a moment, staring at it in disbelief. *You have got to be kidding me! We haven't been home for months and no one has been in our house: how can our sewer be backed up?* I holler for Justin and he is just as shocked as I am. But the how and why will have to wait; we don't have time to do anything but protect Matthew. A warm house with bacteria-filled water standing in it could be deadly to an immune-compromised child. Justin puts Matthew's industrial mask on him while I run to open every window and door.

Our family had barely arrived before they were gone, on their way to my parents' house. I decide to stay behind and deal with the mess. I am too angry to go anyway. While I wait for the plumber, I change into some old clothes to begin cleaning. It's snowing outside and my house is freezing in no time, but I don't dare shut the windows. I begin to try and clean up the disgusting mess, but it seems to be getting worse, not better. Walking over to my neighbors' house in flip-flops and my T-shirt, I'm cold, but not as cold as I should be. She is expecting me: I am going to borrow some fans. *Merry Christmas.*

If only our other troubles were as easy to clean up as a backed-up sewer. After being home only a few weeks, Matthew is sick again. A few days after Christmas, Matthew is admitted to the hospital for what appears to be GVHD of the gut again and within a few days goes from the bone marrow unit to the PICU, and then back to Cincinnati via medevac plane — all in time to ring in the New Year.

Chapter 28

*We can let circumstances rule us, or we can take charge
and rule our lives from within.*

—Earl Nightingale

January 2010

Our flight to Cincinnati is much better than I expected. The flight crew is so kind and reassuring, the flight itself very smooth, and most importantly, I am thankful to be at Matthew's side. I am anxious to get to the hospital because I know this is the best place for him and that we can begin his healing there. A room is waiting for us as Matthew is rolled into the bone marrow unit on a stretcher. I look around and am surrounded by familiar faces. Sadly, it hardly feels as if we left. Within minutes the head of the bone marrow unit comes in, together with two BMT fellows, another BMT doctor and of course Dr. Edwards. They order tests and draw labs. The team goes into action to find out what is going on with Matthew. Things are happening and I know we are in the best place possible.

As I assumed, it is GVHD of the gut again, which means more steroids and another type of monoclonal antibody. I'm not surprised; I basically expected it. GVHD is nothing new for our boys and I am all too familiar with the standard protocol of treatment. The main problem is that these drugs continue to suppress an already suppressed immune system, opening the door for more infections to rear their ugly little heads. However, Matthew responded very well to this treatment in the fall, so we are optimistic he will again. Obviously, no one can say how long we will be here since we can't predict the future, but I am pretty sure we will be here past the date of Andrew's memorial service. Of course we're disappointed, but that is nothing new for us. Justin and I have spent months planning this service and trying to find the best way possible to honor our son. In the worst-case scenario, one of us will stay with Matthew. The best-case scenario is that Mel will come and stay with Matthew. The good news is that I don't have to decide today, and so I won't.

After the six-hour drive, Justin arrives with the same few things we have grown accustomed to living with: sleeping bag and pillow, laptop and clothes. However, this stay will be different; we no longer have our apartment to take refuge in, if even for a few hours. All three of us will be living together in the room, but that's OK because that is all we have left — each other.

"Matthew, how is he?"

"I wish I had better news, but I don't. His tummy pain is getting worse and so is the uncontrollable diarrhea. He is no longer eating, so his weight is dropping quickly. The chest X-ray and CT are both normal and don't show anything in his lungs, which is good, but his nasty cough is still there, so we're remaining vigilant about the cause. At this point we think it might be his primary immune suppression drug — MMF, so we are starting to wean him off it and he will be done with it in a few days."

I pray that that's the reason, because that would be an easy fix — something we could use. There are still numerous blood cultures, stool samples, blood tests and other labs pending so we should have some more answers tomorrow. In addition, Matthew will be having a skin biopsy later today.

Let me state up front and for the record: we are beyond thankful for our wonderful doctor and team at Cardinal Glennon Hospital. They got all of Matthew's files and records here and helped us with our transfer. Of course, we are equally grateful for the amazing team of doctors here in Cincinnati that is working so hard to find the cause and get Matthew feeling better.

But can I just be honest for a minute? Justin and I are tired, angry, frustrated, anxious, worried and just fed up with our lives. We have gone through not one, not two, not three but *four* bone marrow transplants. We have lost one of our children, and as we fight to keep our other one alive, our lives are dictated by tracking what medicine is due next, hiding from germs and staying away from people. We monitor every urine and stool output, check his skin almost hourly and take blood pressures four times a day. Not to mention that we make up excuses day after day for why Matthew must stay away from all his friends.

We continue to take turns sleeping with Matthew because he needs help going to the bathroom with his pumps. It has now been over a year since Justin and I slept in the same bed together. We have spent months away from each other and from our other child.

We have gone through countless doctors, residents and medical students explaining and re-explaining our unique and complicated journey. We are *over* the surgeries, CTs, echos, X-rays, biopsies, pending cultures, PFTs, GFRs, bone marrow biopsies, MRIs, engraftment . . . that's only a partial list.

And how about living in a hospital? Sleeping on a pull-out chair, sharing rooms and communal living areas with random people, finding your food taken, eating out of vending machines and hospital cafeterias day after day, the constant worry of not knowing what is around the corner. Just look at how great Matthew was doing before when all of a sudden the bottom drops out and the next thing you know, we're being flown here by emergency medical plane.

We are simply two people who love each other very much, who desperately wanted these children, to raise them, to love them and to watch them grow up. And now, somehow, one child is dead and the other is fighting to live. We are utterly devastated.

Having to work on Andrew's memorial service while in the hospital caring for Matthew is hard — very hard. While most of the service is planned, it is my eulogy that I want to perfect — is that even possible? From the moment we began planning, I knew I would stand up and speak, but being able to deliver it well is my priority. So I sneak out into the hallway after Matthew is sleeping and practice in front of a few of my BMT moms. They encourage, they listen and they help me.

As I suspected, we will not be getting out in time for Andrew's scheduled memorial service. I kind of knew deep down inside because it just seems to be the way things work out. Justin and I feel very let down. We planned this date months ago when Matthew was doing well. At the time, it seemed like we were being very conservative with his recovery, and besides we have had to wait long enough: almost five months. Andrew deserves this service, and we need to have it! Our grieving process has been largely put on hold, and that is OK because our priority is to do everything possible to save Matthew. But we miss Andrew, and it often feels we are doing him an injustice, as if he was forgotten. We have yet to have a day when we can just wake up and cry, and cry, and cry. Five months after Andrew has died, we long to have his memorial service and we hoped and prayed that Matthew would be home, doing so much better. I have never believed in karma, but at this point, what other explanation is there? I am so angry and disappointed, I just don't have much good to say.

Every time I am in here I swear it will be the last time, yet somehow it's not. Matthew's vitals plummeted, he turned ghostly white, and when the nurse drew some blood for a stat hemoglobin check we saw that it had dropped from 12.4 to 5.3. The initial thought was internal bleeding, perhaps from a perforation of his bowel from the upper and lower endoscopy done a few days earlier. Back to the PICU we went, and with it came all the fear and worry of being there. Is it even worth me trying to explain the rarity of this situation? Matthew has a duodenal hematoma like his brother, yet we have been told that it is an extremely rare side effect of an endoscopy. Does it matter that Matthew's donor was a perfect match of the same sex who was also young? Does it matter that he is young and is healthy, with no active HLH prior to transplant? At this point, I don't care about anything: his current condition, which I need to learn more about so I can speak effectively with his doctors, his latest labs, what medicine is due next, or the other hundred things that keep my mind on overdrive. All I care about right now is the fact that my Baby Andrew is dead, and Matthew is back in the PICU fighting for his life and I can't do anything about it.

Life is really all about perspective. We seem to learn best from the experiences that affect us and our loved ones. Waking up this morning in the PICU to hear Matthew happily chant: "BMT, BMT, BMT," was joy. That's the perspective I was talking about. We are lying next to each other in the hospital bed and I can hear Justin laughing from the chair/bed. Finally, it appears that we might have gotten a break. Who knows for how long, but we'll take it. The last few days Matthew has been making positive strides and today he seems to finally be feeling good, well, good enough that he wants everyone to know he is done with the PICU and ready to head back to the bone marrow unit. Apparently the doctors are in agreement and we will back on the floor by tonight. You have no idea how great it feels to leave this unit. I can feel myself smiling from ear to ear — something I have not done in a while — and it feels wonderful. We just keep laughing at Matthew, he is truly amazing. A more determined, sweet and loving boy there could not be. To think he is so happy just to be getting out of the PICU, not even the hospital! Perhaps, just maybe, now Justin and I will both be able to attend Andrew's memorial service.

Chapter 29

You gain strength, courage, and confidence by every experience
in which you really stop to look fear in the face.
You must do the thing which you think you cannot do.

—Eleanor Roosevelt

March 2010

The days are turning into weeks and the weeks into months. It seems like eons ago that we were home for Andrew's memorial service. It is hard to imagine that Matthew was stable enough for us both to go. Of course, Mel came and stayed with him, which was the ultimate gift, but soon upon our return things went from bad to worse for our Matthew Man. He has had a seizure, been on a ventilator, spent sixteen days in the PICU, is on five different immune suppression drugs and has gained so much weight from the high-dose steroids that none of his clothes fit. There has been speculation about some bigger issues with his kidneys, and yet, all the while, he remains 100% engrafted. Ironically, it was engraftment that we chased so desperately in the beginning with Andrew, thinking that was everything he needed to beat HLH. In the end he died 100% engrafted, but it was the chase through three BMTs that took his life. For Matthew, engraftment has never been an issue, but so many other things have.

Despite all the odds being stacked in his favor, he struggles more and more every day. I try everything in my power to make his days bright, to come up with new crafts, new movies, anything to put even a small smile on his face but it rarely helps because he is usually in too much pain, not to mention depressed beyond words. We have started to discuss the possibility of putting him on an anti-depressant but have held off for now. Part of me is concerned about the side effects of these drugs on young children, although I suppose after all the drugs he has had these would be minor in comparison. But I think more than anything, I am hoping, praying, reaching for a sign that I can help make my son better — that's all I want. I made a calendar and had our child life therapist laminate it. I thought maybe having something visual for Matthew to see would help him.

Together with our medical team we set a preliminary date to shoot for getting discharged back to St. Louis. Of course, there are no guarantees — I know that better than anyone — but at least it is something.

If you can will something to happen then that's what I have been doing — willing Matthew to fight. How I want to scream at the top of my lungs: "THIS IS NOT FAIR!" This time we have been in the hospital from the end of January and now it's March. I don't care about the months living in the hospital, all I care about is the pain, the suffering, the lack of life I see every day in my son's eyes. The doctors have pulled out all the stops to suppress Matthew's immune system to try and quiet his GVHD of the gut. I could never have imagined something so horrific if I were not right here witnessing it.

Matthew remains on the pain pump because of his ongoing stomach pain and cramping. The extreme stooling is unbelievable: he goes every fifteen to thirty minutes around the clock. At his worst, he was stooling between four and five liters a day. He is not taking any food or drink by mouth. Where is it all coming from? It is coming from his gut. The insides of his intestines are raw, red, inflamed and constantly sloughing off. Our routine has been the following: Matthew needs to go, so we disconnect all the leads, pick him up and set him on the bedside commode. He is too weak and in too much pain to stand, so when he is done we help him. We lift him back into bed, reconnect him to all of his leads and sensors, put new heat packs on his tummy, zip him into his sleeping bag, get his blankie and lovies just right, and then he says he has to go again. At first it seemed impossible and we would ask him, "Are you sure?" But we quickly learned that he really does have to go.

His bottom is raw, and he is exhausted. His muscles are atrophied so much that he can barely sit up in bed without help. Where oh where has our Matthew Man gone? It takes all the courage I have not to break down every time he has to go potty. It is breaking my heart and I can barely stand to witness my child endure any more pain.

But somehow, he has slowly and steadily made enough improvement that I have felt confident enough to approach Dr. Edwards with the idea of going home. I know that Matthew is far from well, but I am so worried about his depression that I feel getting him home is almost as important as his medical treatment if he is going to make it long-term. Talking to Dr. Edwards is easy. I am not telling her anything she doesn't know, and if anyone wants us to go home and have some privacy it is her. We agree on a tentative date and I couldn't be happier. Finally something for us to shoot for, to look forward to, to hold on to. We begin crossing the days off every morning and focusing on the big star — our discharge day.

It seems to help a little. Not as much as I was hoping, but I know that once the day comes it will really hit him. I know this day is a huge deal, something that most people in our situation would not get yet. Packing everything up and loading the car is a good feeling — a *great* feeling. Trying to coordinate everything we will need when we get home and preparing the car for the trip is a challenge, but one we are happy to take on. We have to bring enough urinals and pink buckets for stooling for the six-hour drive home, since Matthew can't use a public restroom. Matthew will be leaving the hospital connected to pumps with medicines running. I have a bag packed full of medical supplies for any and all emergencies and a cooler packed with ice to keep certain medicines cold. Going home is going home and we will gladly do it any way we have to.

I don't know what I was expecting, but it was more than what I'm seeing. I so wanted Matthew to be happy, really happy, for the first time in such a long time but he isn't. I can tell he is trying, but he is still a very sick little boy. I am putting all my eggs in the home basket, hoping that being out of here and back in his playroom and bed will make as much difference as it did before. I take one last look around our room to make sure we have everything, although really I couldn't care less if I leave something behind because the one thing I care about in this world is sitting in this wheelchair with a mask on his face, ready to go. Our nurse pulls open our big wooden door, and we are greeted with the most amazing sight: a parade lining the long hall. It is made up of nurses, doctors, therapists and anyone else who is on the floor. Everyone is singing and cheering us on as we push Matthew slowly down the hall, hopefully for the last time. There are lots of tears being shed by everyone, and I am sure, for many reasons. The best part is Brian, the music man, who is singing and playing his guitar. He has handed out other instruments for the staff to play, and it is making quite the sendoff. And then we are loaded into our car and pulling away from our home, Cincinnati Children's Hospital. In some ways it seems like we just got here and in other ways it seems like we never left. Either way, I am thrilled to be going home and can't wait to see my Matthew Man start to come back to life.

The balloons on the mailbox and the gigantic banner that spanned our garage were completely unexpected.

"Look, Matthew, all the kids from the street signed their names and decorated the driveway. Look, Buddy, they are all welcoming you home!" I say, but as I look back at my son I see that he doesn't really care. And why should he? He is very sick and just because we just pulled up in our driveway doesn't mean everything is OK now, but oh, how I wish it was. Justin carries Matthew inside and takes him down to the playroom, his favorite spot. I follow them and help get Matthew comfy and turn on some cartoons. *He is home, finally*, I think to myself. *Home for good.*

Unlike last time we came home, Matthew has not made the fast improvements in his physical strength, and his mood is really lagging behind. He seems to be lost in there and try as I might, I cannot seem to break through. The playroom, the trains, the bunk beds — none of it seems to be helping much. Justin assures me it will just take more time, since he has been so much sicker. Our days remain busy with the nonstop medical care and long clinic visits, but I don't mind. I'm just grateful to be home and able to care for Matthew. Going to clinic for the day will always beat being inpatient. However, today's clinic appointment is not going well and Matthew is in a lot of pain, has developed a fever and is throwing up. *How can this be happening? Why can't my son just get better and stay better?* I am scared.

Chapter 30

There is really nothing more to say-except why? But since why is difficult to handle, one must take refuge in how.

—Toni Morrison

April 2010

T he engines are humming and we quickly take flight. I look out the window and see nothing but lights on the ground as we climb higher and higher into the night sky. I continue to reassure Matthew that everything is OK and Mommy is right here, Buddy. Matthew is being flown back to Cincinnati via their medical plane. He lies there looking at me, holding onto my Andrew Bear lovie while he's hooked up to numerous monitors and getting a blood transfusion. His head rests on his red gingham pillowcase from home. He is quiet and every time I look at him my heart drops.

The doctor they sent from Cincinnati is warm and calming, which is good because I am scared and the bumpy flight is not helping my nerves. It has been another long day from hell. Matthew went from being outpatient in the clinic this morning to being admitted for a fever and then to the bone marrow unit as he got sicker and sicker, and finally to the last stop, the PICU. We had agreed that if Matthew got really sick we would head straight back to Cincinnati, but I really thought we were done with being there. My sweet, sweet Matthew Man. We were only home for two weeks.

Nothing could have ever prepared me for what transpired over the next two weeks. There are no words to begin to explain the horror that took place. Matthew was sick when we arrived and proceeded to get worse and worse. I knew we were going to be here for a while, but planting my feet and digging in is what I had come to do best. I don't scare easily and I will not back down. The only place I had to be is next to my son, helping him get better.

Yet each day seemed to bring more and more challenges. Matthew started to develop some respiratory issues and that of course scared the hell out of me, considering what happened to his brother. After too much struggling we put him on BPAP, positive pressure air ventilation. He sat in his bed in the PICU with a huge mask on his head that blocked his view, but he never complained or tried to pull it off, which he could easily have done. He just sat there watching his Scooby-Doo movies just as he had so many days before.

The tests continued and the answers remained inconclusive. Things just kept getting worse. Before long we found ourselves sitting in one of the rooms off the PICU where doctors take parents to talk about the really bad stuff. Like all the other times I listened and asked questions, and like all the other times I knew this is what we had to do to get Matthew better.

I am not sure how things got so bad so fast. Maybe I had been too busy trying to be strong and stoic and in charge every day during rounds. But all of a sudden I looked around and realized there were twenty-six doctors and nurses standing around Justin and me. Everyone went through their notes and talked about the plans, the progress, the next steps and I stood there in my monogrammed blue-and-white zebra-print nightgown, frozen. Matthew had more machines connected to him than I thought humanly possible, and the ventilator was the least intimidating of them all, if you can believe it. As rounds finished, our PICU doctor put his arm around me and said, "Mom, it is serious. You can cry, it's OK." But what he didn't understand was that if I stopped for one second and let myself cry it would never end.

I went to the chapel that night in the hospital and kneeled and cried and begged God to save my son. But somehow, the perfectly healthy little boy who had never even had HLH, who had a perfect match on the bone marrow registry and who fought with all his might lost his battle and died the most horrific and gruesome death imaginable. I cannot begin to describe what happened in the last few days and hours of Matthew's life, because it is simply too much for me to bear. He looked nothing like himself and that alone broke my heart.

At first I just lay next to him on his bed and cried. I don't remember the details because I was clearly losing part of my mind. After some time, I began to do what I had done just eight short months before with his younger brother. I bathed him and wrapped him up and Justin helped me put him on my lap. We sat there for a long time, holding our son, crying and begging him to forgive us. And then, just like before, it was time to take him down to the morgue. Justin walked next to me as I held my dead firstborn son in my lap. We lifted him up and laid him down on the same cold metal table. We left him with his special lovies and kissed him until I could not stand there anymore and turned to walk away.

And then, just like that, Justin and I stand facing each other in the room where our son has just died. How in the world has this happened? How did we go from two kids to no kids? We are stunned as we look around at our stuff and try to figure out what to do next.

We can't leave town because we have to wait for Matthew's autopsy and cremation, but where are we going to go? I grab my sleeping bag and angrily throw it in the trash. *I won't be needing this thing anymore.* I round up all of Matthew's movies and decide right then to donate them to child life; he would want that.

And then there's nothing left to do but leave. Holding each others' hands for strength, we are just making our way out of the PICU when Dr. Gopal, Matthew's doctor, calls out to us. We stop to talk, hug and cry, and then unexpectedly he unbuttons the top button of his shirt and loosens his tie. He takes his necklace off and hands it to Justin.

"This is the symbol of Om," he explains. "I have worn this for many years, as it was given to me by a very special person. I want you guys to have it. It has brought me a lot of peace and that is what I wish for you." With many more tears we thank him and leave.

Chapter 31

A wife who loses her husband is called a widow. A husband who loses his wife is called a widower. A child who loses his parents is called an orphan. But there is no word for a parent who loses a child.

—Anonymous

May 2010

T he back of my minivan has two empty bucket seats that used to hold two car seats with two children in them. Now they only hold one small urn that contains all that is left of my firstborn son, Matthew Austin Akin. Justin accelerates, and we pull onto the highway, leaving Cincinnati behind as we head west to St. Louis. The only thing I know for sure is that a large chunk of my heart is dead, and I don't think it will be possible for me to live without it. I just keep repeating to myself, *I can't believe this.* As we begin the six-hour drive home, I ponder, *why even go home? What's there that I want?* We pass other cars and I can't help but be envious: they have no idea how lucky they are. I occasionally notice car seats in some of the cars that we pass by, and I just cry harder.

"What are we going to do?" I sob and don't even wait for an answer from Justin. "I don't want to see anyone or do anything, but sitting still is killing me. I want to climb out of my own skin. I cannot believe this. I cannot believe Matthew is dead too. What did I ever do to deserve this?"

I don't know how long we sit in silence, our tears the only sound in the car, until I finally speak again.

"Eight months ago we had an energetic, happy, beautiful son and now he's dead and it's all because of us!" I scream.

"Kristin, please, you know we made this decision based on love and the advice of all the experts. Please don't say that."

"But it's true! If we hadn't taken Matthew to transplant, he would still be here today."

"Maybe, but he could have also gotten a virus that triggered his HLH and died within hours. Either way we were in a horrible position, and you know that. We did everything possible to give him the best chance of survival and sadly things did not go as planned."

"I know . . ." I say. "Justin, I know you're right, but it doesn't help one bit."

My cell phone keeps ringing, but I refuse to answer it. I cannot and will not talk to anyone right now. Everyone knows from our CarePage that Matthew passed away and we are headed home. What else is there to say? In the meantime, I can't stop thinking about Matthew's PICU doctor, Dr. Gopal. We could not have asked for a more compassionate, loving and sympathetic doctor. From our first meeting at the beginning of the week when he came on service, we hit it off immediately. He had the perfect combination of intelligence, patience and humor, something I latch onto quickly. Perhaps humor is not the right word, since there was nothing funny about Matthew's rapidly declining health or the fact that his medical issues had everyone baffled about what the problem was and how to fix it. Yet, somehow there were brief moments when we could find something small to joke about, and that was beyond necessary. The fact that he shared his cell phone number with us, telling us to call any time we needed him during the few hours he wasn't there, spoke volumes about his true intentions: doing what was best for Matthew and for us. I have met more than my fair share of doctors over the past three years and doctors like him are few and far between. I wish we could have met under different circumstances, but then we would not have received the gift that he gave us, which we desperately needed during this horrific time. Despite my heartache and overwhelming desire to just vanish from earth right now, I know that Dr. Gopal was God's gift to us in the midst of hell. His help was the only thing that could get us through what most would call impossible.

"Less than sixty miles to St. Louis," the sign says, and I cry even harder. I don't want to go home. I don't know where I want to go, but the thought of walking into our house without our children is more than I can imagine.

"Maybe we should keep driving," I say to Justin. "I can't bear to see their rooms, all their pictures, the brand-new playroom. I can't do it." But he assures me that it will be OK; it will feel good to be home and have some privacy.

"Besides, Gilligan will be so happy to see us," he adds, knowing that Gilligan was my first "child" before we had our boys. But I can't imagine anything that will make either of us feel better.

As we pull into our neighborhood I find myself ducking down. I don't want anyone to see me; I don't want to make eye contact with anyone. When we pull into the garage the first thing I see is Matthew's bike, and my heart sinks even further into my stomach. But I can hear Gilligan barking as usual, and that brings the first hint of a smile to my face through the tears. There is a plethora of food, cards and flowers sitting on our kitchen island. I look at it briefly, pause and finally walk away. I have no desire to read anything right now. There are no words that can begin to help me and no one understands anyway. I don't want to read a bunch of repetitious rhetoric. I fall to my knees and Gilligan comes over and starts licking me. I take both urns and the kids' special blankets and head upstairs to our bed. I slowly climb in and, holding my sons as tight as possible, cry myself to sleep, hoping to never wake up.

When I wake up it is difficult to open my eyes because they are so swollen from crying. I slowly crawl out of bed and begin to wander aimlessly around the house. At Matthew's doorway I begin crying all over again. I stare at the brand-new bunk beds we had just bought him before his transplant. Justin and I agreed we wanted him to have something fun to look forward to after his transplant. We knew how much he and Charlie would enjoy playing and spending the night together in a bunk bed. We talked about it so much during his recovery; we all longed for that day. But right there next to my son's brand-new bunk bed is the bedside commode that he needed, and that makes me so angry I have to walk away. I look at all the pictures and toys and wonder, *now what? What in the world am I going to do?* Before we even started trying to have children, Justin and I knew that when the time came I would quit my job to be a full-time stay-at-home mom, something we both wanted for our family. And now, somehow, despite the best doctors, the latest medicines, and our unending love and devotion to our sons we are left with nothing. Everything in life seems silly and unimportant now after what we've been through.

Within days of being home Justin and I have to get away. Staying in the house is about to kill us but figuring out where exactly to go is not so easy either. We definitely don't want beach volleyball and cold Coronas, and we're not up for sightseeing either. Justin suggests Miraval, a resort in Tucson, Arizona. He was there many years earlier with his mom and thinks it will be the perfect place.

I am pretty much open to anything anyone suggests because I am so depressed I don't see how I'm going to survive. The only thing I do know is that I don't know how to help myself. I am empty. I simply have nothing left to give anyone, including myself. For thirty-three months my life was consumed by HLH, bone marrow transplants, drugs, tests and procedures — anything and everything to try and save my sons' lives. In the blink of an eye, all my purpose in life is gone; I have nothing and I can't see how I am going to find any purpose again.

Our time spent at Miraval couldn't be better. It is the perfect place for us. We have so many amazing experiences: physical, mental and spiritual. While a lot of it is new to me, I keep an open mind. The resort is located at the base of the mountains out in the desert of Tucson. It is peaceful and serene. Part of this is the location and the small size of the resort, but there is also something unique about it, a special energy. Just being outside every day with the warm sun on our faces is healing after living inside a hospital for so long. Justin and I spend a lot of time talking about our life and what it is going to look like now. We discuss everything from selling our house and moving to a new city to adopting a child.

The one thing we're sure of is that we want to start a nonprofit foundation in the boys' honor. Just talking about the foundation brings us some peace. It is finally something positive after all this sadness. Keeping Matthew and Andrew's memory alive while helping families deal with this awful disease is the best way we know to help ourselves. Brainstorming about the purpose and mission of the foundation is a wonderful distraction.

Chapter 32

And whoever welcomes a little child like this in my name welcomes me.

Matthew 18:5

Summer 2010

"Think about how wonderful it would be if we had another baby," Justin says.

"It just seems too soon," I cry. "I feel bad just talking about it. It's not that I don't want to. Maybe, at some point down the road, but right now I can't manage to think about it."

"Kristin, I realize it's soon, but it takes years to adopt a baby. It's not like we're going to get one all of a sudden. We've agreed that life seems pointless without the boys. You said it best: even though you love me, you don't want to take me to Disney World." I can't help but laugh a little, but it's true. I suppose my fear of being hurt or disappointed is holding me back. At this point I am teetering on the edge, and it wouldn't take much to push me over, unless, of course, I jump first.

I admit, I have no idea what to expect since adoption is something I have never investigated. I don't even know anyone personally who has gone through it. But having more children biologically is not an option for us. After meeting with a world-renowned fertility specialist I thought my head was going to explode. Those big decisions and choices . . . I thought we had finished playing God and I don't ever want to do that again.

I know in my heart that adoption is the right option for us, but it doesn't soothe my feelings of anxiety when we go to meet someone to talk about it. I finally agreed to meet this woman, a friend of a friend who has adopted and helps other families like us. Justin called her and set the whole thing up, and I am just supposed to come with an open mind. We get out of the car and make our way to the country club swimming pool. She is there with her two kids for swimming lessons.

Within the first two or three minutes of meeting each other, the tears are already flowing. We hit it off and start to share our most personal stories; despite being perfect strangers we are connected through the bond of motherhood and our desire for children. Looking back, I could not be more grateful to this woman for helping us with something I didn't know at the time how much we needed. As we finally get up to leave, she hands me her personal binders from both adoptions and tells me to keep them as a resource until we bring our own baby home. I politely thank her, thinking *oh no, that will be way too long, if it even happens. I'll call her in a few weeks and return the binders then.*

The home study is the first step in the adoption process. It is the perfect project for me; a collection of every pertinent and non-pertinent document of your life since you were born, and then some. My type A personality and I go to work with a cute new black-and-white damask pattern three-ring binder, with plastic sheet covers, tabs — the whole works. I begin to gather our history piece by piece. Some of it is easy to find, while other parts take some tracking down, but it comes together and before long all we need is our FBI criminal background checks to come in. And to think anybody can just get pregnant and have a baby! In the meantime, I schedule our personal and in-home interviews with our social worker.

Honestly, I don't mind the interviews, and the paper trail is nothing more than an exercise in organization and following orders, but the thought of putting together some type of personal book to sell ourselves seems, well, a little daunting. I look at many couples' books online, and to be honest, they all look about the same. Talk about overwhelming; how do you go about neatly summing up your life in a little scrapbook? We're all are going to say the same things, and the only thing that is going to separate Justin and me from the crowd might just scare people away. As I begin to make our book, the early days of Justin and me before kids is easy. But what can I say about my two precious children? How can I sum up their lives and deaths in a mere page or two?

But then I realize this book isn't about our children's disease. The pages about Matthew and Andrew need to show one thing, and that is our love. We loved them from the minute we knew they were coming into this world until they took their last breath — and beyond. We will never stop loving them, and that is exactly why we are seeking to adopt in the first place: to share that love again between parent and child that we miss so much.

Our decision to adopt is something that we have only shared with close friends and family. We know it will be a long time, if ever, before we are blessed with a child so we need to keep moving forward without this being our entire focus. As the days pass and turn into weeks since Matthew died, I keep myself busy traveling. I don't think I have been home for more than a week at a time before I am on a plane again, flying somewhere. I suppose the constant motion is a good distraction from reality, for the time being. In addition, Justin and I are busy working on the foundation. But I am starting to realize I still need something else to occupy more of my time.

Out of the blue I get a call from my previous employer about doing some contract work; it could not come at a better time. I go back to work, something I did not foresee but am grateful for nonetheless. Being around other people and having structure and routine is something I desperately need. And it's becoming more and more necessary for me to have a reason to get out of bed. As time passes, my grief and guilt are eating away at me like a slow progressive disease. Depression has a tight grip around my neck and each day it squeezes a little more life out of me.

Labor Day is fast approaching, and that means the first anniversary of Andrew's death, so Justin I decide to get out of town and go visit some friends in Austin, Texas. We don't need an anniversary to be reminded of him dying — not a second goes by we don't think about it — but the anniversary seems especially daunting. As we make our way through the airport, security and finally onto the plane, my eyes are continually wet with tears. Justin and I aren't talking much; there isn't much to say. The flight is easy. I look around at the other people on the plane, wondering what brings them to Austin. I wonder if they're coming here to avoid something like we are. The plane pulls into the gate, I try to touch up my makeup, but it's useless. It's obvious I've been crying. We immediately head out for some dinner — Tex-Mex, Justin's favorite. Sitting outside in the warm, beautiful night is relaxing. Talking and laughing, catching up with friends - it feels good. Justin is right: getting out of town was a good idea.

I snuggle into our cozy guest bed and decide to check my e-mail one last time while I wait for Justin to get out of the shower. He walks in our room and I can barely speak.

"Look at this," I sputter, handing him my phone. I stare at his face while he reads the e-mail. Justin looks up at me, our eyes meet and for once we both have tears of happiness. I reread the e-mail again, trying to absorb what is in front of me. A young mother is due in two weeks and wants to place her baby for adoption. Are we interested in talking to her? My mind is whirling — and for the first time, in a good way. I cannot believe this!

"How in the world am I going to go to sleep tonight?" I laugh. All of a sudden, the thought of this possibility makes me happy and excited. It seems too good to be true.

Despite having a busy weekend lined up, all I can think about is this baby. Is it fate? Is it luck? Is it really a possibility? During the drive from Austin to Houston for a football game we are so excited we have to share it with our friends. As I hear myself talking about it, I get the biggest shock of my life. This is not random chance or even luck: this has been orchestrated by our boys. The e-mail came through on the first anniversary of Andrew's death. It was from a friend; she is an ob-gyn who is the mother of a friend of Matthew's from school. She's not even the birth mother's regular doctor, but she saw her today, they got to talking, and one thing led to another. She mentioned our story and that we were interested in adopting, and said that if the mother was interested, she could help connect us. My tears won't stop — partly because I am in utter shock from this whole event, and partly because I miss the hell out of my boys.

"Do you want me to call her or do you want to?" I ask.

"You call her," Justin says.

"OK, let me get my 'I'm not too anxious to adopt your baby because I realize this is a huge decision for you but I am very interested and would love to have him or her' voice on." My first call gets their answering machine, and I don't leave a message, so when my phone rings from an unknown St. Louis number, I answer it, hoping it's them. The conversation goes well. I do nothing but speak from my heart — that is all I have left. I am honest, I am crying, I am nervous, I am excited. I share our story about the boys and our desire to be parents again.

Most of the talking is between me and the birth mother's mom, as the birth mother is young — still in high school. But we all talk together and I am so impressed with their honesty. Obviously this is a hard situation, but the family has discussed their options and they feel that adoption is best. I admire the courage and maturity it takes to understand that sometimes being a parent means making hard choices. This mom knows that having a baby at her age will be tough, and she realizes that at this time in her life she needs to finish school.

The next few days are a blur. We are busy with our friends in Texas but wondering if we are going to be chosen to adopt a new baby into our home and hearts. We are scheduled to meet Courtney's mom on Tuesday when we get home and give her our profile book. Gosh, all I have is the one copy. I decided I should get one copy and proof it before I order tons and ship them out to adoption agencies all over the country. My mind jumps from *what if they choose us?* to *what if they don't?* I can't stop talking about it, and I think I am going to burst. I desperately want these people to like us, to see that we are good people, that we are loving parents, that we long to be a mom and dad again. But all they have is this book I made on my computer: some color pictures with my summary of our life. How does this read to a perfect stranger? Our book is now in their hands, but I keep worrying.

I can't stop harassing Justin.

"Are they going to choose us? Are they not going to choose us? Do you think it's a girl or a boy? Have you thought about names?"

"Kristin, please stop. Things will work out if they are meant to. Just be patient." How in the world can he be so calm? I call our social worker and fill her in on the last several days, and she advises us to call a private adoption attorney, just in case. By Wednesday night I can't stand the pressure. It's been five days since we first received the e-mail and I finally make Justin call Courtney's mom, just to check in. We are scheduled to fly to L.A. first thing Friday morning, but how can we go when something this big hangs in the balance? At the last minute the attorney's office calls: she has an opening and can fit us in tomorrow afternoon after all. Courtney's mom tells us that the kids have not yet looked through our book together but will tomorrow, and she will call to let us know. I cannot begin to imagine how difficult a situation this must be for these two very young, but brave, people.

The attorney is nice and pretty much what I expect: formal, all business, all legal. She advises us that girls this young almost always change their minds, so don't get too excited. However, if we are chosen after the baby is born, which is not for almost two more weeks, we should give her a call. We decide to grab a bite to eat before heading home — this will give me more time to grill Justin about what he thinks. I know realistically that he has no idea what they are thinking, but I need someone to talk to. I keep playing out every scenario, and Justin keeps telling me, "Just be patient."

Coming home to our empty house I stop and think about what it could be like very soon if we are chosen. Wow, the thought is really more than I can process. Our suitcases are packed and we are just about ready for bed, since we have to get up extra early to catch the first flight out, and then it happens: Justin's cell phone rings.

From his voice, I know within seconds who it is and I feel my heart beat faster. He walks away from me and I stand in our bedroom, frozen, waiting for him to return with the news. Calmly he walks back into our room and I just about tackle him.

"What? What did she say? Did they look at our book? Do they like us? Do they want to meet us?" A huge smile crosses Justin's face.

"Yes," he says. "Timothy came over tonight and they looked at our book together and yes, they like us. As a matter of fact, they have chosen us to be the parents of their child."

"What?" I scream. "Are you kidding me? What, they want us? We are getting to adopt a new baby? I can't believe this!" I cry. Justin grabs me and we hug each other with all our might. He steps back and looks me straight in the eye.

"Oh, and by the way, Courtney went to the doctor today and she had early signs of pre-eclampsia, so they admitted her. She is in labor, and they will call us later tonight or early in the morning when the baby is born!"

A baby is being born right now and we are going to be its parents. I cannot believe this, I simply cannot believe this.

"We're obviously not going to L.A. tomorrow," I laugh. I want to jump up and down and run around and call everyone I know, but what I need to do is go to sleep because I'm going to meet my new baby tomorrow. We unpack and put everything away, as if we were never going anywhere again. We agree to not tell anyone just yet. Lying in bed, trying to fall asleep seems impossible, but then I hear Justin's phone ring. It's morning. I look over at the clock and see it is 7:15 a.m.: this must be Courtney's mom. I sit up and wait impatiently for Justin to hang up.

"He's here. He was born early this morning and is healthy. Courtney is ready to meet us. She wants us to come up to the hospital now." He: it's a baby boy. I am utterly stunned. I get out of bed and into the shower like a robot on automatic.

"What do you wear to something like this?" I ask Justin.

As usual, the tears are flowing, because I am both happy and sad. The hot water feels so good, almost like therapy, as it runs down my back, and I begin to thank my angels for this most amazing gift. Yet I cry because I miss them. What would it be like today if they were here? Would we still be blessed with this new son?

Nothing could have prepared me for the death of my sons Matthew and Andrew. But that is also true of the adoption of my son William: nothing could have prepared me for that.

As I walk into the room that morning I have no idea what to expect. I know everyone has seen our book, but we have only met Courtney's mom once. How do we convey our gratitude for the ultimate gift without looking too excited? How do we show them that this baby will be the light of our life, even though we haven't even seen him yet? How do we assure them that we will spend the rest of our lives loving him, teaching him and nurturing him the best we can? How do support them for making what I imagine is one of the toughest choices they will make in this lifetime?

We introduce ourselves, and after a little while Timothy takes us to the nursery to meet our son for the first time. The nurse wheels him over to the glass so we can see him. He all bundled up: so tiny, so sweet, so beautiful. Tears roll down my checks as I feel my heart start to open again for the first time since my boys died.

Chapter 33

Even hundredfold grief is divisible by love.

—Terri Guillemets

Present

ndrew Preston Akin died September 5, 2009, and his older brother Matthew Austin Akin died just eight short months later, on May 1, 2010. They battled an immune deficiency called hemophagocytic lymphohistiocytosis, underwent four bone marrow transplants in an effort to save their lives, dealt with complication after complication, and finally, after all human effort was expended, they left their physical bodies. I will never get over their deaths, or the pain that they endured. The images and details will haunt me forever. A part of me died when they died and that is my reality. I miss them every single day and would give everything in my power to bring them back.

But the fact is, I can't. Whether I sit around and have a pity party for the rest of my life or get up and do something positive, either way they are not coming back. So I chose to move forward and hopefully make them proud. Of course, some days are easier than others. There are days when I wake up and think, *I can do this. I can take on this disease and help people and make a difference.* But those days are often followed by days of tears, anger and bitterness. I look at everyone with their healthy kids and am full of envy. I think, *let someone else make a difference. My kids are dead; I deserve to do nothing.* I often tell people, "Just because you didn't see me cry today doesn't mean I didn't." And that's OK. I don't think you ever get over the loss of a loved one, especially a child; you just learn how to live with it. I chose to let my boys love guide me, not let their death define me.

When Andrew died I was devastated, but I put all I had left into saving Matthew. When Matthew passed away I truly felt that my life was over. As time passed things only got worse. I could not imagine living another thirty or forty years without either of my children. I had started to give serious thought to suicide. Why not? Who could blame me? I had even started to write the letter.

But lo and behold, God stepped in and did what He had so many times throughout our journey: He gave me an unbelievable gift, just as He had done so many times before during this journey. It was exactly what I needed. Many people thought it was too soon; I myself even wondered, but it was clearly the ultimate gift from my boys. And so despite the fact that Justin and I have lived through every parent's worst nightmare — twice — the gift of William solidified my faith. A brand-new healthy baby, and we were given the astonishing gift of being his parents. William is love, and with love anything is possible. We are never promised an easy life — in fact our lives here on earth are full of hardships and lessons. But if Matthew and Andrew had never gotten sick, we would never have started a foundation to support children with HLH and their families, we probably never would have adopted, and we would have been content just going through the motions of life. We would never have pushed ourselves to see that we are stronger than we realize. As Peter Marshall says: "When we long for life without difficulties, remind us that oaks grow strong in contrary winds and diamonds are made under pressure."

Our hearts and minds have been opened and changed, and we often tell people that despite our horrific experiences, the lessons we have learned have been invaluable. We see the world in a way most people never will, and we realize we are fortunate in that. We are put on this earth for a purpose, and often that purpose is very different from what we want or plan for. But if we can be open to the big picture, then we will surely be rewarded with the big prize. There is no doubt that life is not fair, and why bad things happen to good people will remain a question to be debated for years to come. But I have learned that the best way to help myself is to help others.

Soon after the boys died I went back to my weekly volunteering at the Ronald McDonald House. I had started there years ago, back in Dallas before we moved to St. Louis and had kids. Being there allows me to help others who are in similar situations, facing the struggles of a critically ill child. Anything I can do to help makes me feel good because I know the horror firsthand. In addition, Justin and I have been very busy since the inception of The Matthew and Andrew Akin Foundation. Brainstorming and working together to develop our mission is good therapy for us. It helps us channel our grief. Talking about ways to honor the boys, raise awareness, and raise money are all much better than dwelling on what happened to them. I don't want people to remember them by their death but rather by the good work we do in their names.

We remain humbled by the gift of our son William. He is the funniest and most joyful little toddler. Not surprisingly, he has many similarities to his brothers but is completely his own person, hence his name Will-I-am. He is a gift that was sent directly to us, and not a day goes by that we forget that. Thankfully he has been the picture of health, and that too is something I thank God for daily. We can't imagine our life without him and the only thing I regret is that I don't have him and Matthew and Andrew, but I know that is not how it was supposed to be.

People have asked us, "Do you love him as much as your other boys?"

I find it shocking that someone would have the gall to suggest that I wouldn't love him as much, but I quickly and easily answer: "Yes, of course I love William as much, because he is as much mine as Andrew and Matthew are." Don't they see? Had Matthew and Andrew been long-term survivors, the only thing they would not have had was our DNA, and the only thing that William doesn't have is our DNA. Like I said, he is ours and our love is the same — perhaps deeper, because we now know how precious and fragile life really is. Most importantly, I know that by taking a chance, by opening my heart despite my fear and pain, I have learned that love does trump grief.

I don't know what the future holds for me, so I remain flexible. I will go where I am led. I'm enjoying being a stay-at-home mom to William. Running errands together, playing outside and just doing the normal things is wonderful. I keep busy with our foundation and my regular volunteer work. I just want to make a difference, I want to help others and most importantly I want people to know that if your worst nightmare comes true, as mine did, you can still make it.

I know that my boys are alive and well. They send me special messages to let me know they are OK and that they are near. But that story is for another day. Just remember: "While we try and teach our children all about life, our children end up teaching us what life is all about."

Lessons Learned

1. No one belongs to us - not our children, spouse, family or friends. They are simply on loan: use your time wisely.

2. Doctors and medicine offer options, but beware; nothing comes for free.

3. We are all stronger, braver and more resilient than we realize.

4. Do not wait or hesitate - tell whoever you love, that you love them.

5. Take more pictures and video. Pictures are great, but video is priceless.

6. Be flexible. Don't let circumstances outside your control dictate your life. Make what you want to happen, happen.

7. Like it or not, you must be an advocate for a sick loved one.

8. Always seek the experts.

9. Grief never goes away. It becomes like a disability, something you learn to live with and manage a little better each day. But that doesn't mean you like it.

10. Love is the essential ingredient in everything in life. Give love, share love, spread love.

MATTHEW *and* ANDREW

AKIN

F O U N D A T I O N

BUILDING ON BROTHER'S LOVE.

(501c3 charitable foundation)
11503 St. Charles Rock Road
Bridgeton, MO 63044

Proceeds of *Love Trumps Grief* and donations to The Matthew and Andrew Akin Foundation provide resources to families of children dealing with HLH and going through the bone marrow transplant process, fund HLH research and educate the public on the importance of joining the National Marrow Donor Program.

CPSIA information can be obtained at www.ICGtesting.com
Printed in the USA
BVOW01s0808110414

350168BV00001BB/242/P

9 781457 512568